Critical Thinking Activities • Intermediate

Brain Teasers

by Carol Eichel

Teacher Created Materials, Inc.

P.O. Box 1040
Huntington Beach, CA 92647
©1993 Teacher Created Materials, Inc.
Made in U.S.A.

ISBN 1-55734-490-6

Edited by
Amy LasCola

Illustrated by
Keith Vasconcelles

TABLE OF CONTENTS

INTRODUCTION

Brain Teasers provides ways to exercise and develop brain power! Each page stands alone and can be used as a quick and easy filler activity. The pages can be distributed to students as individual worksheets or made into transparencies for presentation to the entire class at once. The book is divided into sections so the teacher can find activities related to a subject being taught or to a particular student's needs. The activities are especially useful in helping students develop:

- Logic and other critical thinking skills.
- Creative thinking skills.
- Research skills.
- Spelling skills.
- General vocabulary skills.
- An understanding of the regionalized language of Western culture.

FAMOUS PAIRS

Name these famous persons' counterparts.

Batman and   _____

Lewis and   _____

Romeo and   _____

_____ and Mr. Hyde

_____ and Jerry

_____ and Lois Lane

Mark Antony and   _____

Mickey and   _____

Barbie and   _____

_____ and Jill

_____ and Olive Oyl

_____ and Josephine

Orville and   _____

Blondie and   _____

Hansel and   _____

PICK A PAIR!

List items that are sold in pairs.

1. _____
2. _____
3. _____
4. _____
5. _____
6. _____
7. _____
8. _____
9. _____
10. _____

11. _____
12. _____
13. _____
14. _____
15. _____
16. _____
17. _____
18. _____
19. _____
20. _____

WORD PAIRS

Write the missing half of each word pair.

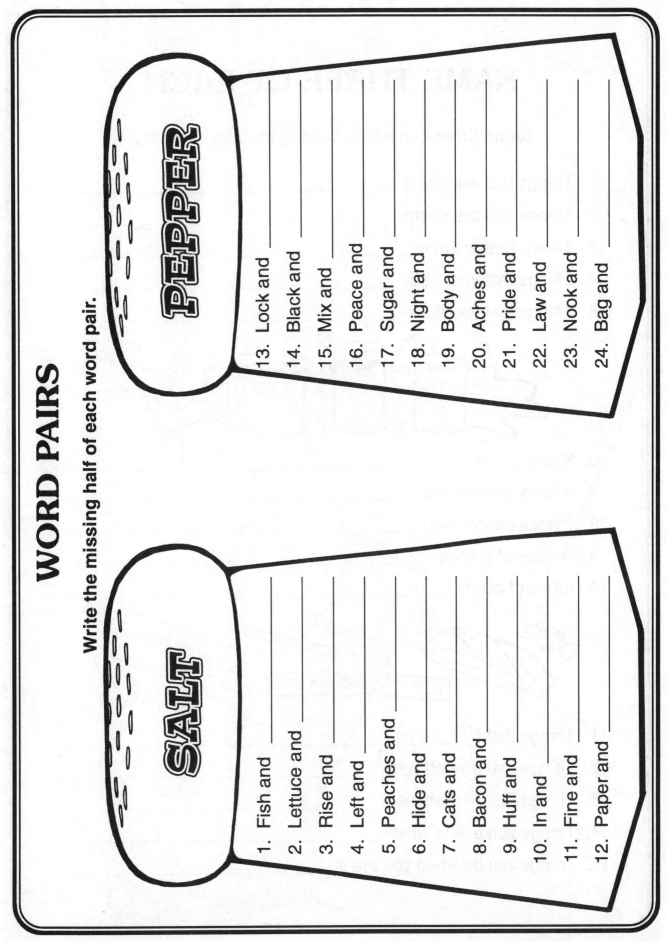

SALT

1. Fish and _____
2. Lettuce and _____
3. Rise and _____
4. Left and _____
5. Peaches and _____
6. Hide and _____
7. Cats and _____
8. Bacon and _____
9. Huff and _____
10. In and _____
11. Fine and _____
12. Paper and _____

PEPPER

13. Lock and _____
14. Black and _____
15. Mix and _____
16. Peace and _____
17. Sugar and _____
18. Night and _____
19. Body and _____
20. Aches and _____
21. Pride and _____
22. Law and _____
23. Nook and _____
24. Bag and _____

NAME THREE OF EACH

Name three items that belong to each category.

1. Things that are round _____

2. Things that are sharp _____

3. Things that are blue _____

4. Things that you read _____

5. Things that you drink _____

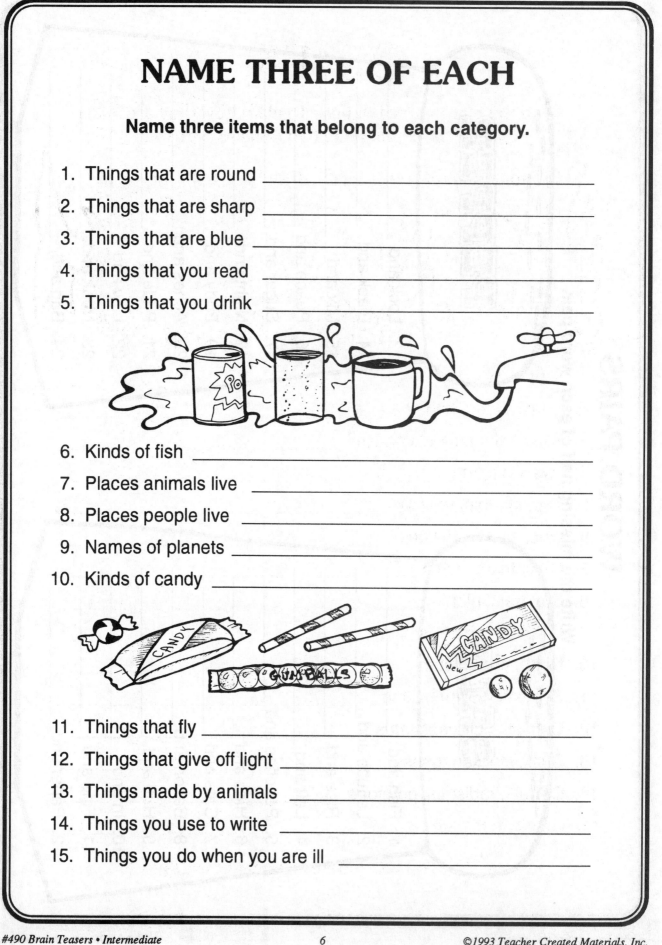

6. Kinds of fish _____

7. Places animals live _____

8. Places people live _____

9. Names of planets _____

10. Kinds of candy _____

11. Things that fly _____

12. Things that give off light _____

13. Things made by animals _____

14. Things you use to write _____

15. Things you do when you are ill _____

ALL ALIKE

**Read the words on each line. Explain how they are alike.
An example has been done for you.**

Octopus, shark, eel   __animals who live in the water__

1. Red, yellow, blue _____
2. Sorry, proud, happy _____
3. Yogurt, ice cream, cheese _____
4. Jog, walk, run _____
5. Trio, triangle, tricycle _____
6. One, seven, eleven _____
7. Iowa, Idaho, Ohio _____
8. Car, train, plane _____
9. Europe, Asia, Australia _____
10. North, west, south _____
11. September, April, June _____
12. Cumulus, cirrus, stratus _____
13. Duck, chicken, goose _____
14. Carrots, radishes, potatoes _____
15. Cradle, bed, bunk _____

Extra: Can you add words to some of the lines?

WHICH ONE DOESN'T BELONG?

In each line below, one of the four words doesn't belong with the other three. Circle the one that doesn't fit. Explain what the others have in common. An example has been done for you.

Africa, North America, Europe, (England) ___Continents___

1. Nephew, uncle, niece, father _____

2. Dictionary, math, atlas, encyclopedia _____

3. Rose, daisy, tomato, carnation _____

4. Chicken, pig, cow, horse _____

5. Pen, chalk, eraser, marker _____

6. Lion, kid, cub, lioness _____

7. Lightning, rain, sun, dark clouds _____

8. Red, yellow, blue, green _____

9. Orange, lemon, watermelon, grapefruit _____

10. Reds, Dodgers, Cowboys, White Sox _____

11. Laugh, giggle, chuckle, cry _____

12. Bread, butter, muffin, bagel _____

13. Blood, liver, heart, kidney _____

14. Relish, hot dogs, mustard, ketchup _____

15. California, Oregon, Washington, Kansas _____

THE GREAT ESCAPE

At the farm last night, the animals (one was a bull) got out of the barn. Help Mr. Owens get them back in their stalls.

1. The goat is in either the first or last stall.
2. The pigs are in either the first or last stall.
3. The sheep are next to the pigs.
4. The cow is in the stall before the horse and not next to the pigs.
5. The horse is in the third stall.

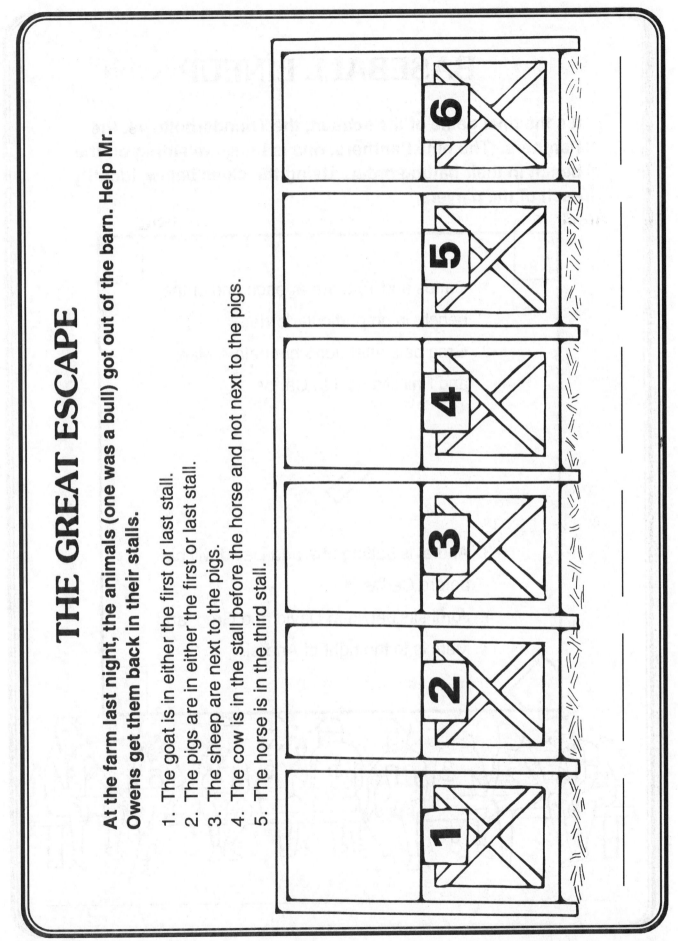

BASEBALL LINEUP

It's the final game of the season, the Thunderbolts vs. the Panthers. The nine Panthers, one is Luis, are sitting on the bench in their batting order. Using the clues below, identify each of the players.

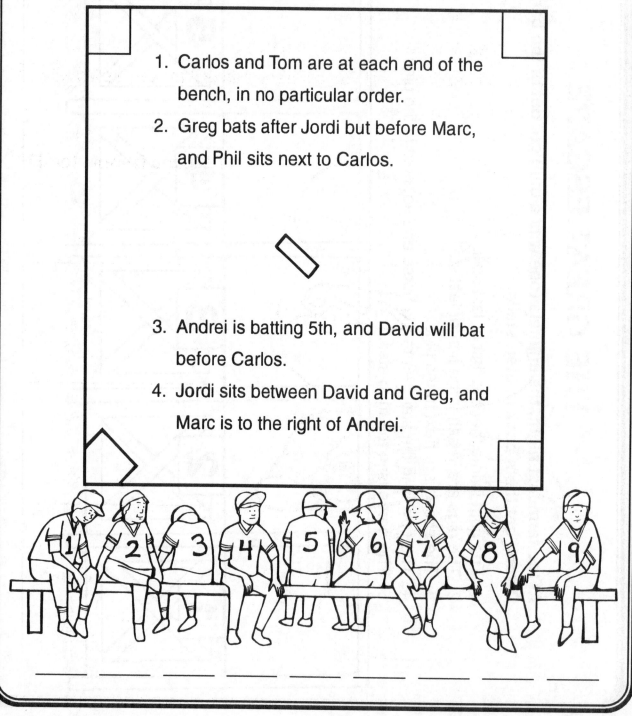

1. Carlos and Tom are at each end of the bench, in no particular order.

2. Greg bats after Jordi but before Marc, and Phil sits next to Carlos.

3. Andrei is batting 5th, and David will bat before Carlos.

4. Jordi sits between David and Greg, and Marc is to the right of Andrei.

FAVORITE FOODS

The favorite foods of Megan, Michael, Sergi, and Jana are pictured below. Each person has a different favorite food. Use the following clues to match the people with their favorite foods.

1. Michael likes ketchup and mustard on his favorite food.

2. Jana is allergic to cheese.

3. Sergi eats his favorite food on a bun.

4. Sometimes for something different, Michael makes his favorite food into corn dogs.

Whose favorite food?

_____

_____

_____

_____

RICHEY'S DOG

Richey wants a dog for his birthday. When Richey and his parents arrive at the pet store, five dogs, one is a dachshund, greet them with barks and yips. Using the clues below, determine which dog belongs in what cage and which dog Richey chooses.

1. The greyhound is next to the pug.

2. The cocker spaniel is lapping up water in the middle cage.

3. There are no cages to the right of the pug.

4. The pug and collie are at opposite ends of the pet cages.

5. Richey chooses the puppy in the first cage.

BLACK OUT

Black out every letter that appears two times or more. The letters that are left will spell out the answer to the following riddle:

What is a monster's favorite summer drink?

```
Y J B Q C Z F W M X B J M F
G N X K N R E B V J C R Z P
B C P Y Z W F T K N E M V S
Z H J R N Q C B E N M Q P F
E V F T J Y Z F T W C B X J
M B C N Q F S E J M P Z C N
S F K Z O Y U E E B W C J S
J N E C V B R Y N Z K W V N
Z V F X T F Q J C L P Y B C
J S B N M E Y C T X Z C M Q
M Z C E B J S F M P B R F S
B C N M Q W J V Y K A V X Z
Z E F C R P B M J T N N I C
M R J Z S N C W E F P M Q B
R B T R K Z Q E C S Y K N E
S E F W Y X T P Z C B X R D
Z M Q V B M F B J E J S V T
```

PALINDROME WORD FIND

Palindromes are words, phrases, sentences, or numbers that read the same forward and backward. An example is noon. See how many palindromes you can find in this word find.

```
R R W M B W B B U Y F M R E W E Q P U
L D P A A C O I D F N U N T R H N H T
E O I E C B Q A B J T M M O E A B T V
V T M Y E P D K P K N L T A O N H I U
E O O J X P M G M O R I Q D D N E A U
L O W T U W N I T R Q M Q H O A E T S
B T J P S R N U Y Z K B R S T H M V T
N A D D B D R R Z P L J O O U Q O J E
J Z S O Z I A S H V O H E L T R Z O O
D E E D M G D B A Q S P W O C O Z X T
X Y B O O M A G K A A L P S I K R A T
T E Q B M R R G W D G Z F R V G V B O
E A R K N L S L O I A L U P I K O O C
R E P A P E R U W D S N I O C M L T O
R K H Y O X P R M J N E N T E R K G G
E O J A F O I U X K P M B A C E B I S
T H A K D J N N X R G G E Z C A O T Q
S E E S U Y G D A W Z P B H A B D T W
W L S R D S S P J A V E S C P F N M G
```

SCHOOL DAYS WORD FIND

The word SCHOOL appears 44 times in the word find below.
Circle it each time you find it.

```
S S C H O O L J U K S U T L O O H C S
W C C H J P T S S F C O S S T M B S H
S S H H T D L C C F H S C C N S C E Q
S C H O O L Z H H H O C H H H H S L L
P H H J O O U O O X O H O O O O O T O
W O S O T L L O O L L O O O B O O U O
S O C G O X P L L O T O L L H P P L H
C L H M S L O O H C S L G C A I M F C
H S O B C A B B N U C Q S C H O O L S
O L O O H C S S S C H O O L A S D G T
O B L X O L I C A S O F S H V C S X S
L S B I O V Q H S C O S M C L H C C C
N N C O L Z L O C H L G C O H O H P H
S D H H W O H O H O C M O H Z O O V O
S C H O O L V L O O V H D K O L O G O
S S C H O O L H O L C A F L D O L L L
S E C H U M L I L S C H O O L W L U O
X S K O L S C H O O L S C H O O L V K
```

ANIMAL WORD FIND

Try to find all of the 30 animals hidden in this word maze.

```
A A R D V A R K I S S M O L A E S
C A M O L R A B B I T O M O W L U
A E A G L E A R L Y C H E E T A H
T O G L U E B A B O O N O L O H U
O G O T J A G U A R U N A E X W R
H I P P O P O T A M U S L P O T T
C R H O X L A H N U T L E H T X U
I A E P L A T E A L L I G A T O R
R F R Z E B R A C A N O N N H F T
T F E R R E T X O W N N I T E O L
S E R F I C K A N G A R O O N O E
O A L A O K A N D Y M U S K R A T
T O E I G U A N A T S U R L A W E
W A N A R O U M I P P O C U E L R
```

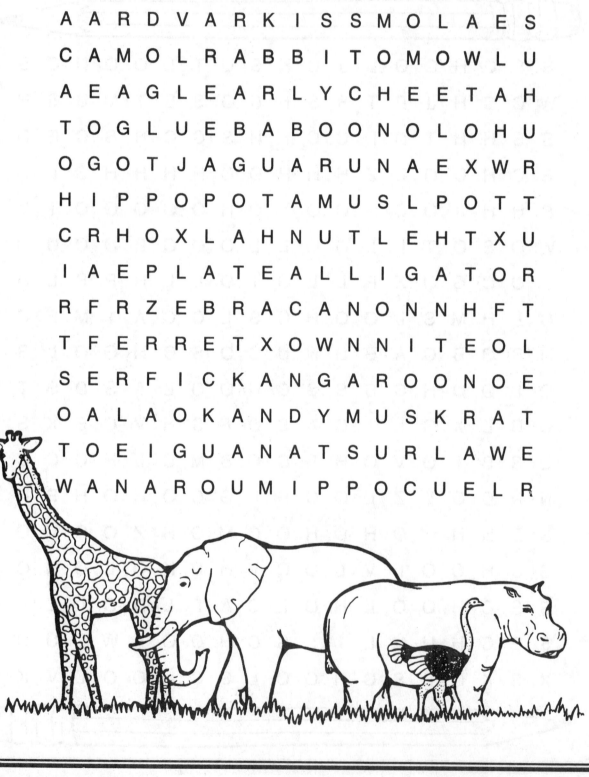

MIXED FRUIT

The names of 25 different fruits are hidden in this word find.
Circle them when you find them.

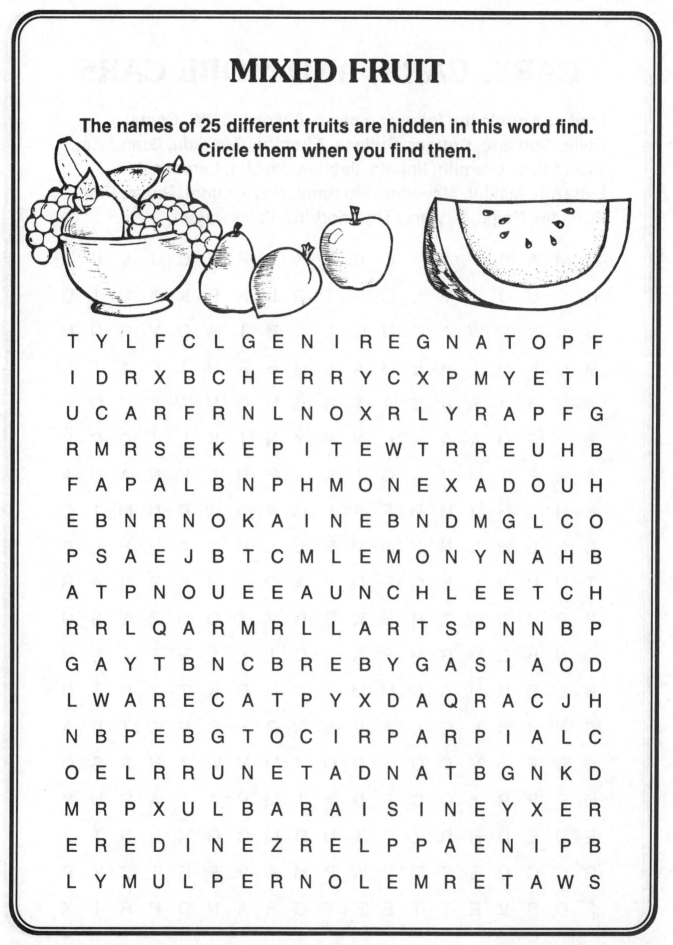

```
T Y L F C L G E N I R E G N A T O P F
I D R X B C H E R R Y C X P M Y E T I
U C A R F R N L N O X R L Y R A P F G
R M R S E K E P I T E W T R R E U H B
F A P A L B N P H M O N E X A D O U H
E B N R N O K A I N E B N D M G L C O
P S A E J B T C M L E M O N Y N A H B
A T P N O U E E A U N C H L E E T C H
R R L Q A R M R L L A R T S P N N B P
G A Y T B N C B R E B Y G A S I A O D
L W A R E C A T P Y X D A Q R A C J H
N B P E B G T O C I R P A R P I A L C
O E L R R U N E T A D N A T B G N K D
M R P X U L B A R A I S I N E Y X E R
E R E D I N E Z R E L P P A E N I P B
L Y M U L P E R N O L E M R E T A W S
```

CARS, CARS, AND MORE CARS

Find and circle the following cars: Accord, BMW, Camaro, Civic, Corvette, Cougar, Cutlass, Firebird, Granada, Grand Am, Grand Prix, Gremlin, Impala, Jaguar, Javelin, Lamborghini, LeBaron, Malibu, Maverick, Mustang, Nova, Omni, Pacer, Pinto, Porsche, Regal, Skylark, Thunderbird, Volkswagen.

```
M M A P T A X C B N X Y P F D J V P A
N J U O J V L O D T O L X R K A G I O
B A X S W I O U C L X B I W D V R N M
M G K G T R E G A L G B A U I E A T N
W U J A S A S A Y R E H G N W L N O I
B A S M A A N R N R Y N I K L I D C P
A R F T M J C G I K I H R L E N A U A
K H X H A D P F S L G A A W B U M T C
B F L U L N V O M R L A B C A H F L E
T U U N L P G E O Y A O V V R P S A R
P P H D W Z R B K S R V X O O Z T S U
O N H E M G M S A A C I L L N T Z S B
R L O R H A R M M I D H B K T Z R T D
S N J B L C L A V E W O E S V W T B A
C B F I V C C I N O Y M M W T H P S Q
H P P R I O C F B A I M P A L A R U Y
E D E D R R Z C T U D M C G K N N T J
R C O Q S D M C W P M A V E R I C K P
C O R V E T T E E Y G R A N D P R I X
```

SHADOWS

Identify each of the following objects by looking at its shadow.

1. _____

2. _____

3. _____

4. _____

5. _____

6. _____

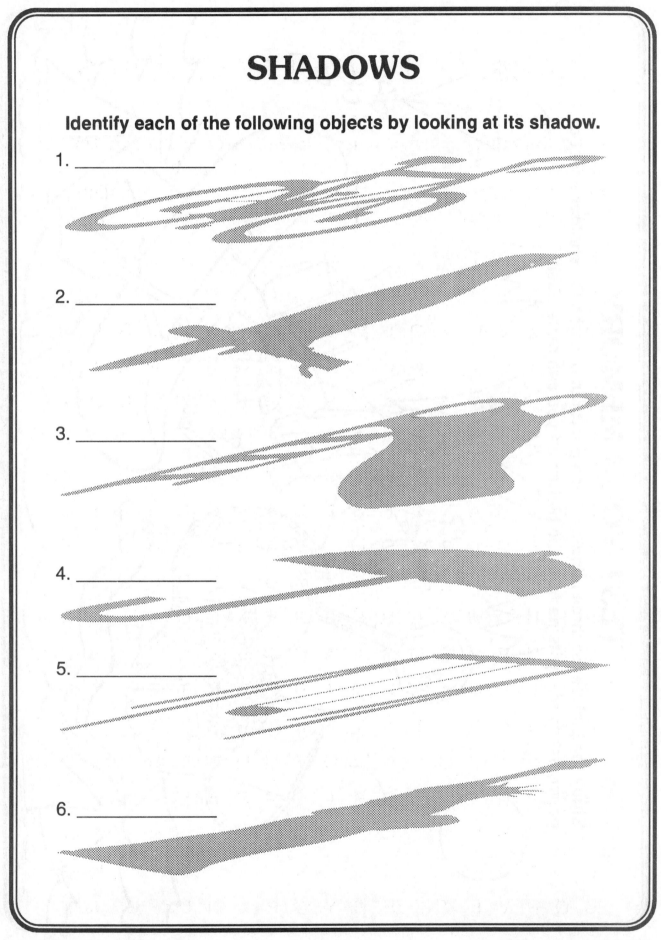

TEST YOUR MEMORY

Study the picture for three minutes. Then put it out of sight. On another sheet of paper, list as many items from the picture as you can remember.

WHAT'S THE QUESTION?

Write a question for each of the following answers.

1. _____

   At 10:30.

2. _____

   A hot dog.

3. _____

   No!

4. _____

   64.

5. _____

   Red roses.

6. _____

   Not today, maybe tomorrow.

7. _____

   Red, white, and green.

8. _____

   In a minute.

9. _____

   Yes!

10. _____

    About 50.

11. _____

    We did!

12. _____

    In 1992.

HIDDEN MEANINGS

Explain the meaning of each box.

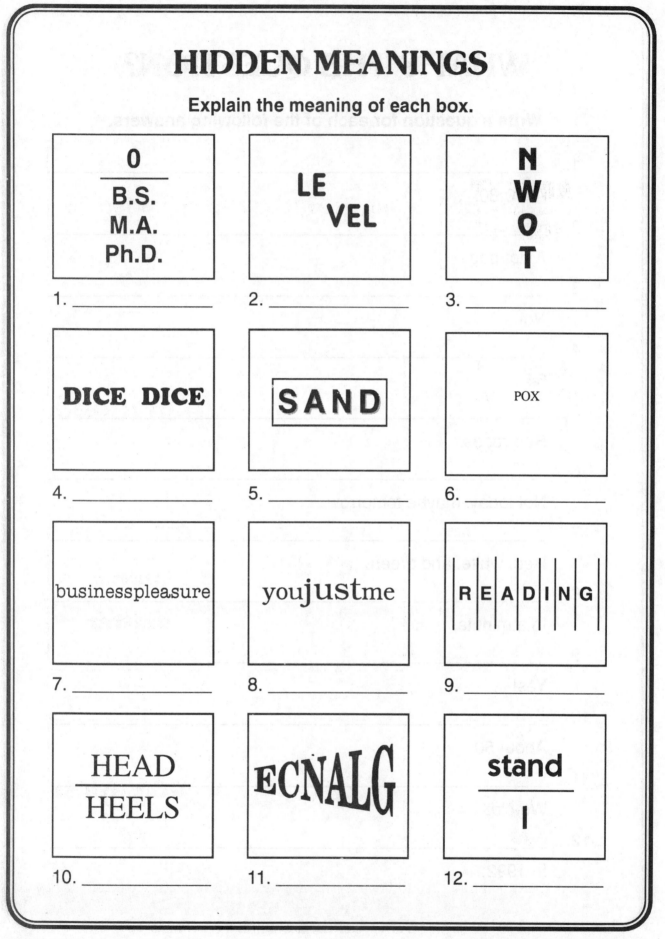

$$\frac{0}{\text{B.S. M.A. Ph.D.}}$$

1. _____

LE
VEL

2. _____

N
W O
T

3. _____

DICE DICE

4. _____

SAND

5. _____

POX

6. _____

businesspleasure

7. _____

youjustme

8. _____

R E A D I N G

9. _____

$$\frac{\text{HEAD}}{\text{HEELS}}$$

10. _____

ECNALG

11. _____

$$\frac{\text{stand}}{\text{I}}$$

12. _____

MORE HIDDEN MEANINGS

Explain the meaning of each box.

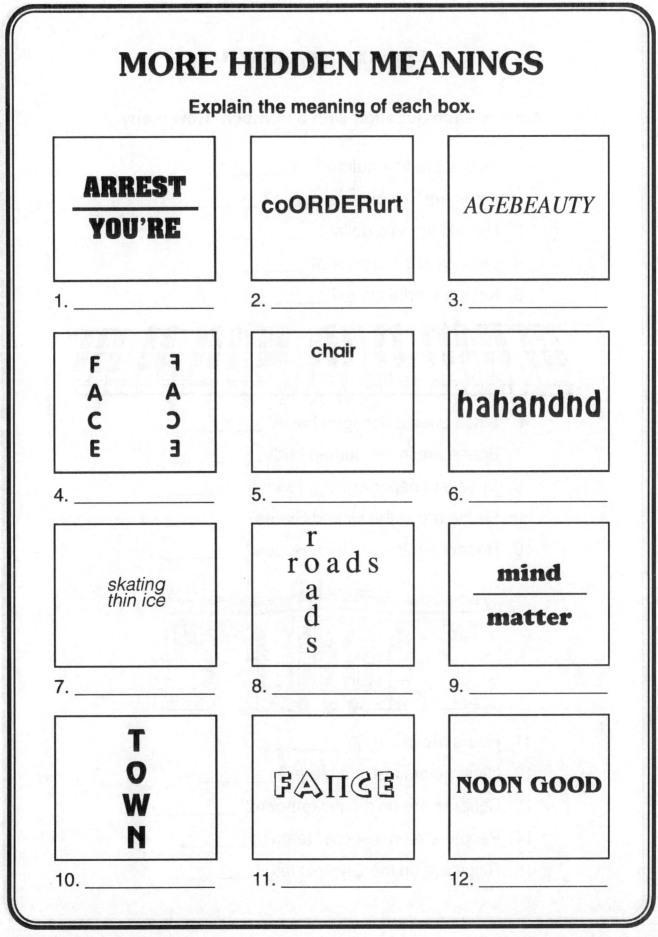

ARREST / YOU'RE

1. _____

coORDERurt

2. _____

AGEBEAUTY

3. _____

FACE FACE (reversed)

4. _____

chair

5. _____

hahandnd

6. _____

skating thin ice

7. _____

r o a d s (roads)

8. _____

mind / matter

9. _____

TOWN

10. _____

FANCE

11. _____

NOON GOOD

12. _____

HOW MANY?

Answer each question with a number. How many...

1. Voices are in a quintet? _____

2. Items are in a baker's dozen? _____

3. Nickels are in a dollar? _____

4. Ounces are in a pound? _____

5. Keys are on a piano? _____

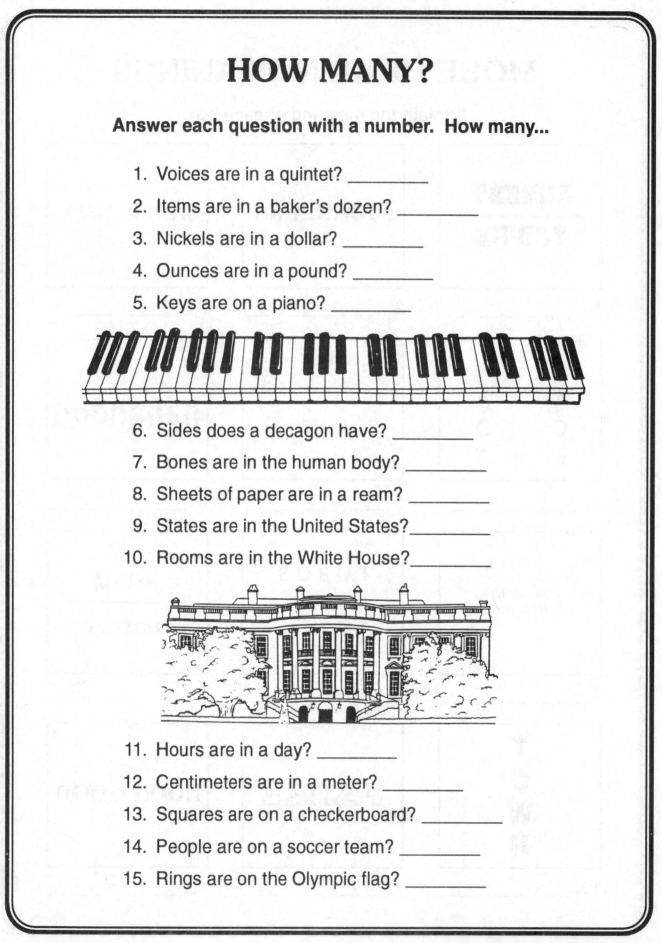

6. Sides does a decagon have? _____

7. Bones are in the human body? _____

8. Sheets of paper are in a ream? _____

9. States are in the United States? _____

10. Rooms are in the White House? _____

11. Hours are in a day? _____

12. Centimeters are in a meter? _____

13. Squares are on a checkerboard? _____

14. People are on a soccer team? _____

15. Rings are on the Olympic flag? _____

ADDITION AND SUBTRACTION

Place + and - signs between the digits so that both sides
of each equation are equal.

1. 3   2   1   4   1   3   =   10

2. 8   7   1   4   4   6   =   4

3. 5   3   2   4   1   5   =   14

4. 2   1   8   9   3   5   =   20

5. 5   3   4   4   2   9   =   9

6. 7   6   2   9   9   3   =   0

7. 4   9   3   7   3   1   =   19

8. 9   8   6   3   5   1   =   6

9. 3   5   3   9   6   5   =   13

10. 5   1   1   3   4   7   =   17

NUMERAL - INITIAL EQUATIONS

Each equation below contains the initials of words that will make it complete. Find the missing words. An example has been done for you.

$7 = D$ in a W   7 days in a week

1. $1 = V$ in a S _____

2. $2 = P$ in a Q _____

3. $3 = T$ in a T _____

4. $4 = Q$ in a G _____

5. $5 = T$ on a F _____

6. $9 = P$ on a B T _____

7. $9 = P$ in the S S _____

8. $12 = E$ in a D _____

9. $16 = T$ in a C _____

10. $36 = I$ in a Y _____

11. $50 = S$ in the U S _____

12. $66 = B$ in the B _____

13. $88 = K$ on a P _____

14. $144 = I$ in a G _____

15. $206 = B$ in your B _____

16. $360 = D$ in a C _____

17. $640 = A$ in a S M _____

18. $1000 = M$ in a L _____

19. $2000 = P$ in a T _____

20. $5280 = F$ in a M _____

CHANGE PLEASE!

There are over 100 ways to make change for a dollar. List the coins you would give each person below as change for $1.00.

1. Ivan wants 4 coins for his $1.00.

   _____

2. Linda wants 7 coins for her $1.00.

   _____

3. Brian wants 13 coins for his $1.00.

   _____

4. Marcus wants 3 coins for his $1.00.

   _____

5. Jennifer wants 8 coins for her $1.00.

   _____

6. Misa wants 26 coins for her $1.00.

   _____

7. Karouch wants 5 coins for his $1.00.

   _____

8. Yun-Ho wants 6 coins for her $1.00.

   _____

9. Rob wants 10 coins for his $1.00.

   _____

10. Benita wants 14 coins for her $1.00.

   _____

TIMELY CHORE

Each word in the Time Box refers to a specific time span. List the words in order from the shortest time span to the longest. Then explain how long each time span is.

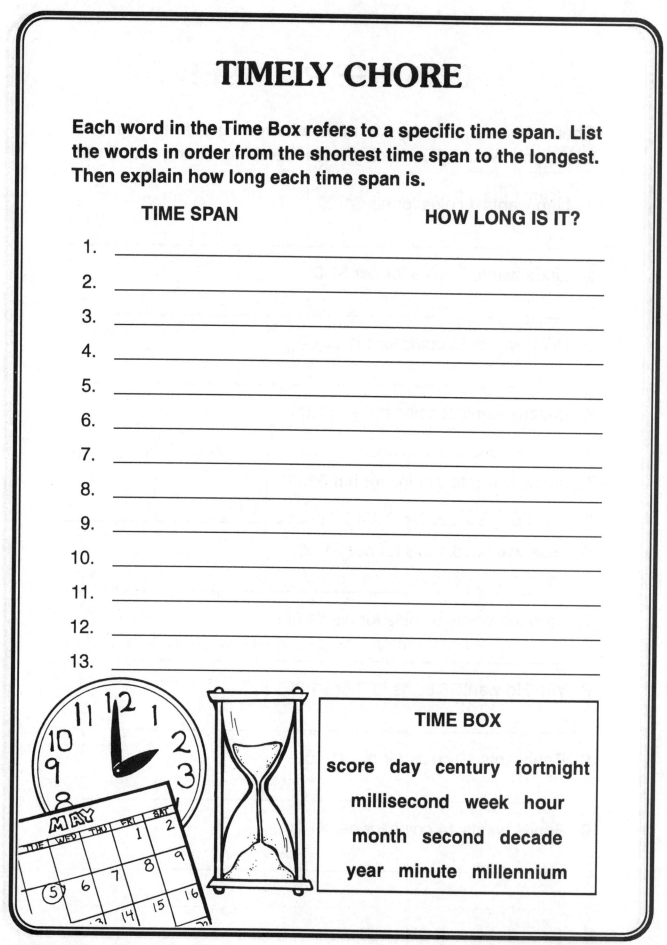

TIME SPAN   HOW LONG IS IT?

1. _____

2. _____

3. _____

4. _____

5. _____

6. _____

7. _____

8. _____

9. _____

10. _____

11. _____

12. _____

13. _____

TIME BOX

score   day   century   fortnight

millisecond   week   hour

month   second   decade

year   minute   millennium

NAMES AND NUMBERS

1. Name the 7 dwarfs in *Snow White*. _____
    _____

2. Name the 4 figures carved into Mt. Rushmore. _____
    _____

3. Name the 5 senses. _____
    _____

4. Name the original 13 colonies. _____
    _____
    _____
    _____

5. Name Santa's 9 reindeer. _____
    _____

6. Name the 2 planets with no moons. _____
    _____

7. Name the 6 colors of the rainbow. _____
    _____

8. Name the 3 cities where the U.S. capital has been located.
    _____

9. Name the 12 provinces and territories of Canada. _____
    _____
    _____
    _____

10. Name the 9 planets in the solar system. _____
    _____
    _____

THE VALUE OF WORDS

In the Value Box, each letter of the alphabet has been given a dollar value. To find the value of a word, add the values of all the letters. For example, the word "school" would be worth $72. (19 + 3 + 8 + 15 + 15 + 12 = 72) Write words with appropriate values in each of the boxes below.

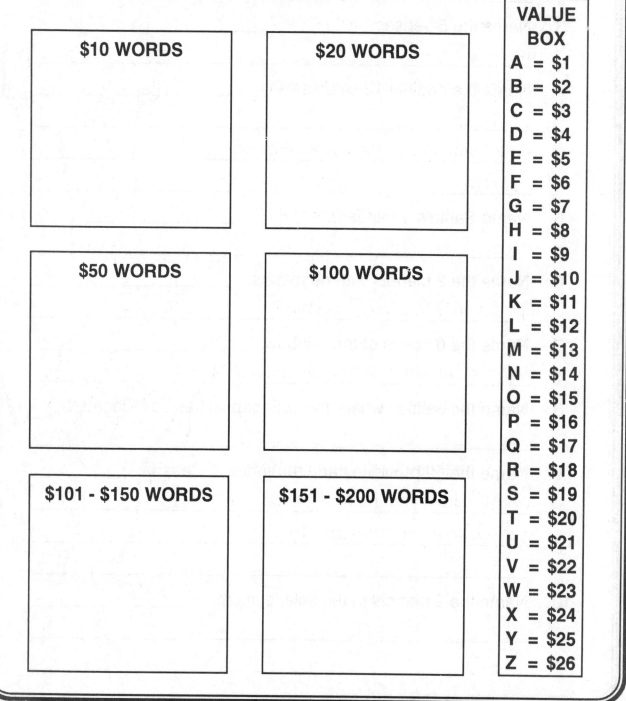

VALUE
BOX
A = $1
B = $2
C = $3
D = $4
E = $5
F = $6
G = $7
H = $8
I = $9
J = $10
K = $11
L = $12
M = $13
N = $14
O = $15
P = $16
Q = $17
R = $18
S = $19
T = $20
U = $21
V = $22
W = $23
X = $24
Y = $25
Z = $26

$10 WORDS

$20 WORDS

$50 WORDS

$100 WORDS

$101 - $150 WORDS

$151 - $200 WORDS

DO YOU KNOW?

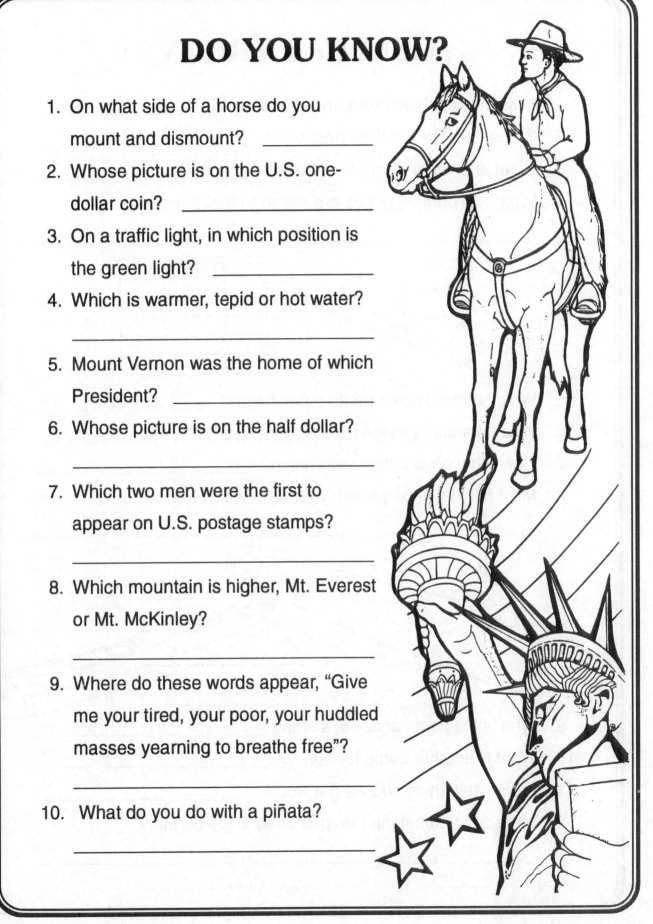

1. On what side of a horse do you mount and dismount? _____

2. Whose picture is on the U.S. one-dollar coin? _____

3. On a traffic light, in which position is the green light? _____

4. Which is warmer, tepid or hot water?

   _____

5. Mount Vernon was the home of which President? _____

6. Whose picture is on the half dollar?

   _____

7. Which two men were the first to appear on U.S. postage stamps?

   _____

8. Which mountain is higher, Mt. Everest or Mt. McKinley?

   _____

9. Where do these words appear, "Give me your tired, your poor, your huddled masses yearning to breathe free"?

   _____

10. What do you do with a piñata?

    _____

GENERAL TRIVIA

1. How many sides does a snowflake have? _____

2. Whose picture is on the penny? _____

3. What is another name for a bison? _____

4. What two primary colors are mixed to make orange?

_____

5. Which bird is known for its beautiful tail? _____

6. What is another name for a moving staircase? _____

7. How often does a leap year occur? _____

8. Most fairy tales begin with what four words?

_____

9. Who is the commander of a ship? _____

10. What is another name for fall? _____

11. From what animal do we get wool? _____

12. What can a submarine do that other ships cannot?

_____

TALLEST, LARGEST, FASTEST

What is the...

1. Tallest living thing? _____

2. Tallest building? _____

3. Tallest mountain? _____

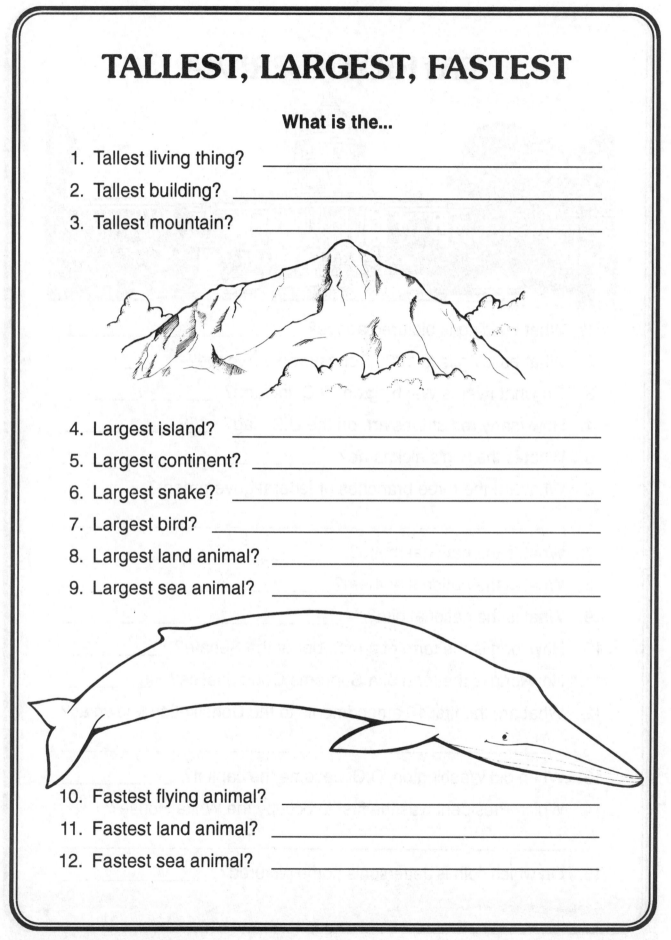

4. Largest island? _____

5. Largest continent? _____

6. Largest snake? _____

7. Largest bird? _____

8. Largest land animal? _____

9. Largest sea animal? _____

10. Fastest flying animal? _____

11. Fastest land animal? _____

12. Fastest sea animal? _____

PATRIOTIC TRIVIA

1. What building is pictured above? _____

2. What building is at 1600 Pennsylvania Avenue? _____

3. On what river is Washington, D.C. located? _____

4. How many red stripes are on the U.S. flag? _____

5. What is the flag's nickname? _____

6. What are the three branches of federal government?

   _____

7. What is the national motto? _____

8. What is the national anthem? _____

9. What is the national bird? _____

10. How long is the term of a member of the Senate? _____

11. How long is the term of a Supreme Court Justice? _____

12. What are the first 10 amendments to the Constitution known as?

    _____

13. When did Washington, D.C. become the capital? _____

14. Which President was the first to occupy the White House?

    _____

15. On which coin is Jefferson's home pictured? _____

PRESIDENTIAL TRIVIA

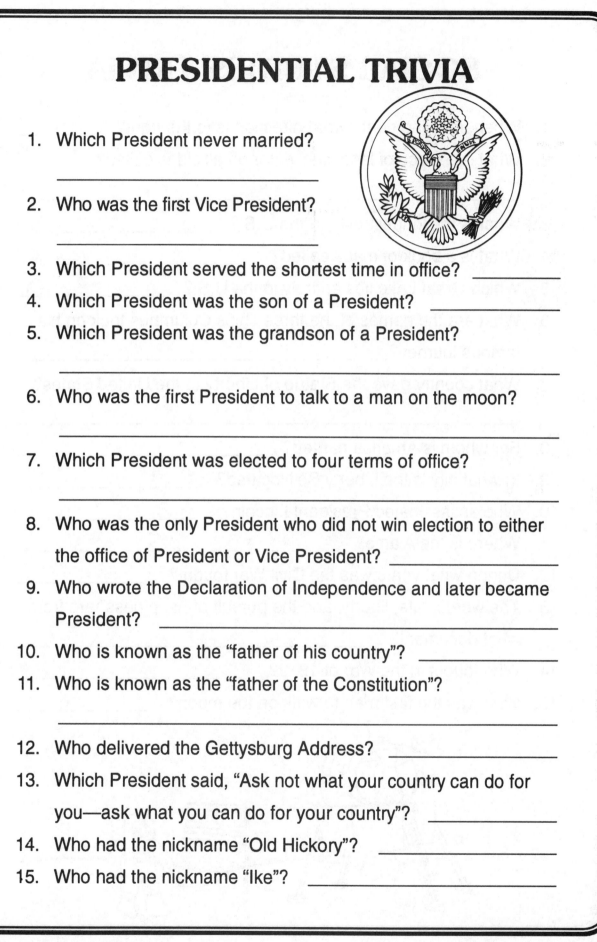

1. Which President never married?

   _____

2. Who was the first Vice President?

   _____

3. Which President served the shortest time in office? _____

4. Which President was the son of a President? _____

5. Which President was the grandson of a President?

   _____

6. Who was the first President to talk to a man on the moon?

   _____

7. Which President was elected to four terms of office?

   _____

8. Who was the only President who did not win election to either the office of President or Vice President? _____

9. Who wrote the Declaration of Independence and later became President? _____

10. Who is known as the "father of his country"? _____

11. Who is known as the "father of the Constitution"?

    _____

12. Who delivered the Gettysburg Address? _____

13. Which President said, "Ask not what your country can do for you—ask what you can do for your country"? _____

14. Who had the nickname "Old Hickory"? _____

15. Who had the nickname "Ike"? _____

SOCIAL STUDIES TRIVIA

1. When traveling north, what direction is to the right? _____

2. What is a piece of land with water on all sides called?

   _____

3. What is the longest river in the U.S.? _____

4. What is a book of maps called? _____

5. Which Great Lake lies entirely in the U.S.? _____

6. What are the names of the three ships Columbus took on his

   famous journey? _____

7. What country gave the Statue of Liberty to the United States?

   _____

8. For whom is America named? _____

9. In what city is the Liberty Bell located? _____

10. Who assassinated President Lincoln? _____

11. Where is the Alamo? _____

12. During what years was the Civil War fought? _____

13. The words, "life, liberty, and the pursuit of happiness" are from

    what document? _____

14. Who fought in the War of 1812? _____

15. Who was the first man to walk on the moon? _____

SCIENCE TRIVIA

1. What instrument is used to measure temperature?

   _____

2. What system of the body is made up of the brain, the

   spinal cord, and the nerves? _____

3. What does the pulse measure? _____

4. What are animals without backbones called?

   _____

5. With what does a fish breathe? _____

6. In what sea creatures are pearls found? _____

7. What is the term for the remains of things found in rock?

   _____

8. What instrument is used to view things that are far away?

   _____

9. Which is the fifth planet from the sun? _____

10. What is Earth's path around the sun called?

    _____

11. What is Earth's natural satellite? _____

12. Which comet is visible every 76 years? _____

13. What is larger, a solar system or a galaxy?

    _____

14. In what three forms can matter exist?

    _____

15. What instrument is used to measure air pressure?

    _____

ENGLISH TRIVIA

? . , ; ! ' : " " ( ) ? . , ; ! ' : " " ( )

1. What words are used to describe verbs? _____

2. In the book *Charlotte's Web*, what is the spider's name?

   _____

3. What do we call a person who writes books, stories, or poems?

   _____

4. What do we call stories that are made up rather than true?

   _____

5. Who wrote *Superfudge*? _____

6. What is the name of the ancient Greek man who wrote a group

   of fables? _____

7. What is a story about your own life called? _____

8. What was Mark Twain's real name? _____

9. What do we call words that mean the same or nearly the

   same? _____

10. Meg, Jo, Beth, and Amy are the main characters in what

    famous book? _____

11. What type of book is based on facts? _____

12. What words name a person, place, or thing? _____

13. What are the two main parts of a sentence?

    _____

14. What punctuation mark is used in a contraction? _____

15. Who wrote the books about Ramona? _____

PALINDROMES

Palindromes are words, phrases, sentences, or numbers that read the same forward and backward. Write a palindrome that relates to each word or phrase below. An example has been done for you.

midday   noon

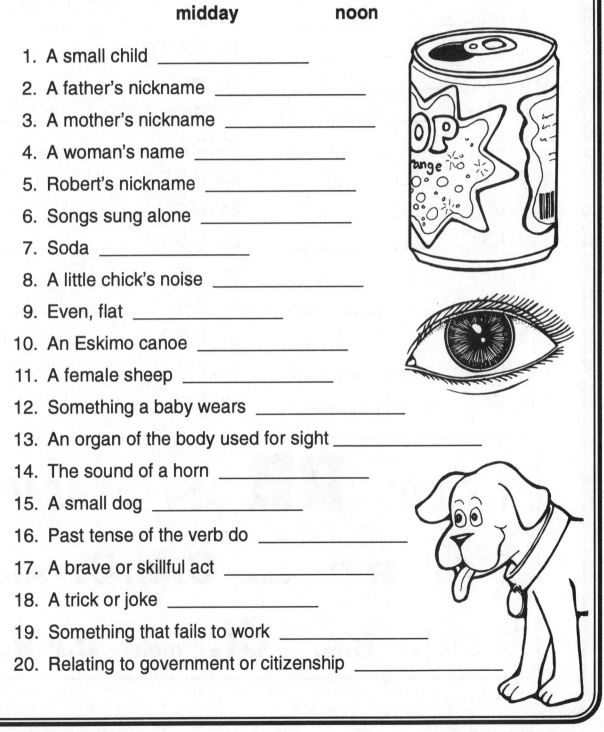

1. A small child _____

2. A father's nickname _____

3. A mother's nickname _____

4. A woman's name _____

5. Robert's nickname _____

6. Songs sung alone _____

7. Soda _____

8. A little chick's noise _____

9. Even, flat _____

10. An Eskimo canoe _____

11. A female sheep _____

12. Something a baby wears _____

13. An organ of the body used for sight _____

14. The sound of a horn _____

15. A small dog _____

16. Past tense of the verb do _____

17. A brave or skillful act _____

18. A trick or joke _____

19. Something that fails to work _____

20. Relating to government or citizenship _____

ABBREVIATIONS

Write the meaning of each abbreviation.

1. St. _____
2. C.O.D. _____
3. bldg. _____
4. lbs. _____
5. P.O. _____
6. misc. _____
7. oz. _____
8. A.M. _____
9. pkg. _____
10. IOU _____
11. Hwy. _____
12. Dept. _____
13. mph _____
14. N/A _____
15. V.P. _____

16. ASAP _____
17. mfg. _____
18. B.A. _____
19. S.A.S.E. _____
20. etc. _____
21. RR _____
22. D.A. _____
23. C.E.O. _____
24. M.D. _____
25. R.S.V.P. _____
26. e.g. _____
27. B.C. _____
28. C.P.R. _____
29. FYI _____
30. esp. _____

R.S.V.P. RR IOU e.g. ASAP

FYI M.D. misc. C.E.O. lbs.

bldg. B.A. St. mph C.P.R.

ACROSTICS

Acrostics are word puzzles or poems in which the first or last letters of each line form a word or words. In the examples below, the first letters of each line form the words school and homework. Complete the acrostics by writing a phrase or sentence on each line that begins with the letter given and relates to the subject, either "school" or "homework."

S _____

C _____

H _____

O _____

O _____

L _____

H _____

O _____

M _____

E _____

W _____

O _____

R _____

K _____

RHYMING WORD PAIRS

Find an adjective that rhymes with a noun so that together, the two words have about the same meaning as the phrase that is given. An example has been done for you.

a comical rabbit   funny bunny

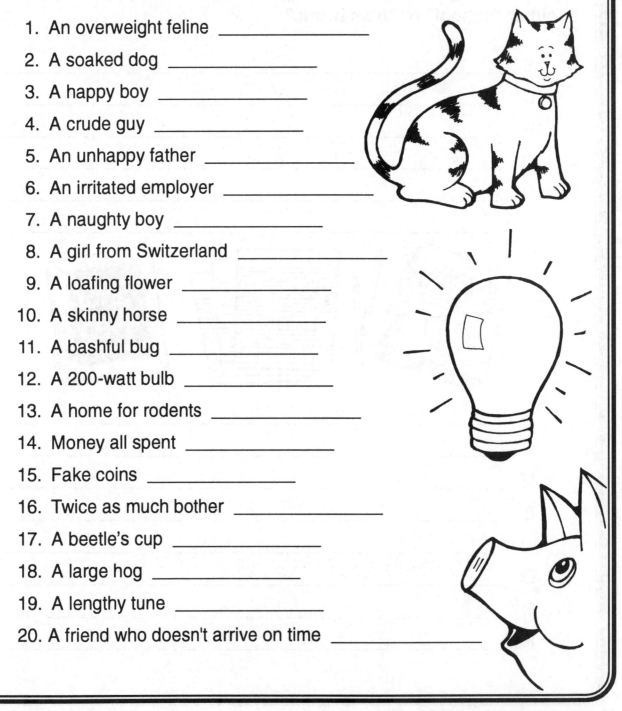

1. An overweight feline _____

2. A soaked dog _____

3. A happy boy _____

4. A crude guy _____

5. An unhappy father _____

6. An irritated employer _____

7. A naughty boy _____

8. A girl from Switzerland _____

9. A loafing flower _____

10. A skinny horse _____

11. A bashful bug _____

12. A 200-watt bulb _____

13. A home for rodents _____

14. Money all spent _____

15. Fake coins _____

16. Twice as much bother _____

17. A beetle's cup _____

18. A large hog _____

19. A lengthy tune _____

20. A friend who doesn't arrive on time _____

WORD CHAIN

Use the last two letters of the first word in the word chain to begin the next word. Continue throughout the chain.

1. The capital of Hawaii   Honolulu

2. The midday meal   l u _ _ _

3. A building for worship   _ _ _ _ _ _

4. A close friend   _ _ _ _

5. A device for protection from rain   _ _ _ _ _ _ _ _

6. A crisscross pattern   _ _ _ _ _ _

7. 1/100 of a meter   _ _ _ _ _ _ _ _ _ _

8. The wearing away of land   _ _ _ _ _ _ _

9. A quick glance   _ _ _ _ - _ _ _ _

10. To rub out   _ _ _ _ _

11. A period of the year   _ _ _ _ _ _

12. On one occasion only   _ _ _ _

13. One hundred years   _ _ _ _ _ _ _

14. A boy's name   _ _ _ _

15. To reply to   _ _ _ _ _ _

16. To stamp out   _ _ _ _ _ _ _ _ _

17. The speed at which a piece of
    music is played   _ _ _ _ _

18. A Mexican cloak, like a blanket   _ _ _ _ _ _

19. The capital of Hawaii   Honolulu

COMPETITIVE WORD CHAIN

Two or more players start at the same time. The object is to fill in all the blanks with a 3-, 4-, 5-, or 6-letter word, depending on the number of blanks given. Each word must begin with the last letter of the preceding word. The first word may start with any letter. (Words may not be repeated.) The first player to complete all the words wins.

1. _ _ _

2. _ _ _ _

3. _ _ _ _ _

4. _ _ _ _ _ _

5. _ _ _ _ _

6. _ _ _ _ _

7. _ _ _

8. _ _ _ _

9. _ _ _ _ _

10. _ _ _ _ _ _

11. _ _ _ _ _

12. _ _ _ _

13. _ _ _

14. _ _ _ _

15. _ _ _ _ _

16. _ _ _ _ _ _

17. _ _ _ _ _

18. _ _ _ _

19. _ _ _

WORD WINDERS

**Use the clues to help you fill in the blanks and circles.
Only the circled letters change from one word to the next.**

1. Antonym for hot   c   o   l   d
2. A pony   c   o   l   ◯
3. A stroke of lightning   ◯ — — —
4. Courageous   — — — ◯
5. Without hair   — ◯ — —
6. Object used in a soccer game   — — — ◯
7. Device that rings   — ◯ — ◯
8. Item worn around the waist   — — — ◯
9. To soften by using heat   ◯ — — —
10. To shed skin   — ◯ — —
11. A fine, furry growth of fungi   — — — ◯
12. A small burrowing animal   — — — ◯
13. An empty space   ◯ — — —
14. To hang on to something   — — — ◯
15. A yellow metallic element   ◯ — — —
16. To bend and crease   ◯ — — —
17. What you eat   — — ◯ —
18. One who lacks good sense   — — — ◯
19. Object used to do work   ◯ — — —
20. A place to swim   ◯ — — —

ONE WORD PLUS ANOTHER

Add one word to another word to make a third word.

1. A male offspring _____ plus something used to catch fish _____ make a form of poetry _____.

2. A rodent _____ plus a shade of brown _____ make a plant used to make furniture _____.

3. A vegetable _____ plus an edible kernel _____ make a seed that ripens underground and is usually roasted before being eaten _____.

4. Male adults _____ plus the highest playing card _____ make a threat _____.

5. A large body of water _____ plus a male child _____ make a period of time _____.

6. A man's name _____ plus a male child _____ make the name of a U.S. President _____.

7. The antonym of on _____ plus frozen water _____ make a place for business _____.

8. A water barrier _____ plus a writing utensil _____ make a verb that means "to make slightly wet" _____.

9. An lightweight bed of canvas _____ plus 2,000 pounds _____ make a type of fabric _____.

10. The nearest star _____ plus the antonym of wet _____ make an adjective meaning "various, several" _____.

WHAT'S THE MESSAGE?

Use the "phone code" to spell out messages for these famous persons.

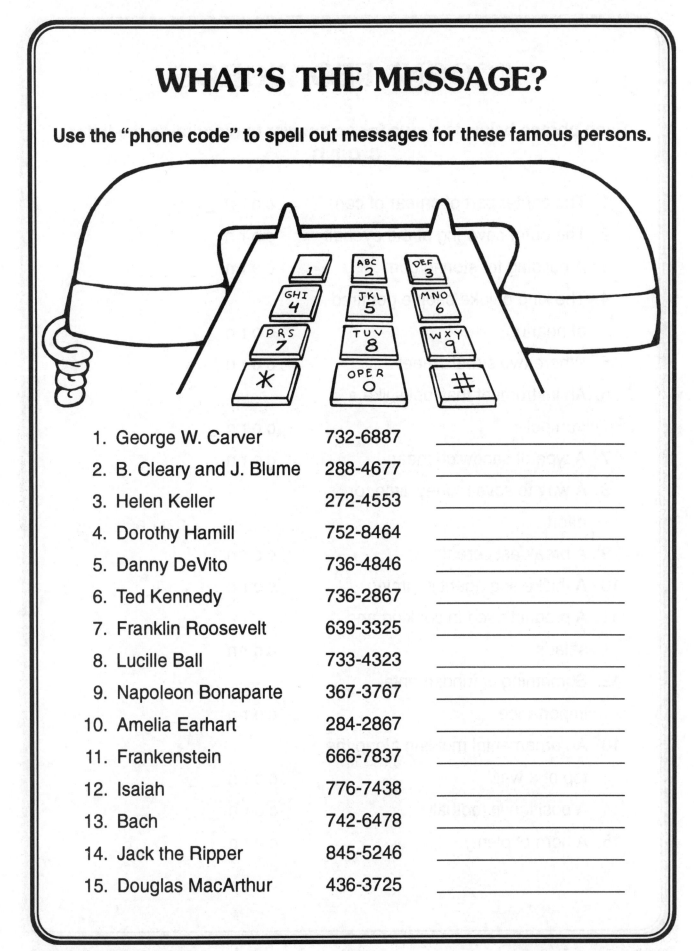

1. George W. Carver   732-6887   _____

2. B. Cleary and J. Blume   288-4677   _____

3. Helen Keller   272-4553   _____

4. Dorothy Hamill   752-8464   _____

5. Danny DeVito   736-4846   _____

6. Ted Kennedy   736-2867   _____

7. Franklin Roosevelt   639-3325   _____

8. Lucille Ball   733-4323   _____

9. Napoleon Bonaparte   367-3767   _____

10. Amelia Earhart   284-2867   _____

11. Frankenstein   666-7837   _____

12. Isaiah   776-7438   _____

13. Bach   742-6478   _____

14. Jack the Ripper   845-5246   _____

15. Douglas MacArthur   436-3725   _____

"CORN"-FED WORDS

Each phrase below is a clue for an answer that contains the letters
c o r n.

1. The center part of an ear of corn   c o r n _ _ _

2. The outer covering of the eyeball   c o r n _ _

3. A building for storing corn   c o r n _ _ _ _

4. The kind of joke people get tired
   of hearing   c o r n _

5. Where two streets meet   c o r n _ _

6. An instrument that looks like a
   trumpet   c o r n _ _

7. A type of sandwich meat   c o r n _ _   _ _ _ _

8. A way to save money, time, or
   effort   _ _ _   c o r n _ _ _

9. A breakfast cereal   c o r n _ _ _ _ _ _

10. A thickening agent in gravy   c o r n _ _ _ _ _ _

11. A product used in cooking and
    salads   c o r n   _ _ _

12. Something of fundamental
    importance   c o r n _ _ _ _ _ _ _

13. An ornamental molding along the
    top of a wall   c o r n _ _ _

14. A position in football   c o r n _ _ _ _ _

15. A horn of plenty   c o r n _ _ _ _ _ _

"FAR" OUT

Each phrase below is a clue for an answer that contains the letters f a r.

1. Good-by   f a r _ _ _ _ _

2. A paid worker on a farm   f a r _   _ _ _ _

3. Remote   f a r _ _ _ _

4. A minor league club   f a r _   _ _ _ _

5. A former British coin of little

    value   f a r _ _ _ _ _

6. One who raises crops   f a r _ _ _

7. Not closely related to the topic   f a r - _ _ _ _ _ _ _

8. Having widespread influence   f a r - _ _ _ _ _ _ _ _

9. The price of a bus ride   f a r _

10. Humor based on ridiculous

     happenings   f a r _ _

11. To overstep reasonable limits   _ _   _ _   _ _ _   f a r

12. Up to this point all is well.   _ _   f a r   _ _ _ _ _ _

13. At a greater distance   f a r _ _ _ _

14. A region of Asia   F a r   _ _ _ _

15. A litter of pigs   f a r _ _ _

THIS "ORE" THAT

Each phrase below is a clue for an answer that contains the letters
o r e.

1. A state in the U.S.   O r e _ _ _

2. A routine task   _ _ o r e

3. Woods   _ o r e _ _

4. To breathe loudly during sleep   _ _ o r e

5. Opposite of less   _ o r e

6. A seasoning used in cooking   o r e _ _ _ _

7. Animals that eat only meat   _ _ _ _ _ _ o r e _

8. In a plentiful amount   _ _ _ o r e

9. The finger next to the thumb   _ o r e _ _ _ _ _

10. To choose not to pay attention   _ _ _ o r e

11. To predict the weather   _ o r e _ _ _ _

12. To love or worship   _ _ o r e

13. An ancestor   _ o r e _ _ _ _ _

14. Took an oath   _ _ o r e

15. Land next to a body of water   _ _ o r e

"PET" PEEVES

Each phrase below is a clue for an answer that contains the letters p e t.

1. Part of a flower   p e t _ _

2. Small, tiny   p e t _ _ _

3. A floor covering   _ _ _ p e t

4. A flower   p e t _ _ _ _ .

5. Liquid used to make gasoline   p e t _ _ _ _ _ _

6. Turned to stone   p e t _ _ _ _ _ _

7. An underskirt   p e t _ _ _ _ _ _

8. A formal request, often signed
   by a large number of people   p e t _ _ _ _ _

9. A naval officer   p e t _ _ _ _ _ _ _ _ _

10. A figure controlled by the
    movement of strings or hands   _ _ _ p e t

11. Small amounts of money for
    incidental expenses   p e t _ _   _ _ _ _

12. Occurring again and again   _ _ p e t _ _ _ _ _ _

13. A man's name   P e t _ _

14. A shallow glass container
    used to prepare cultures in
    science labs   p e t _ _   _ _ _ _

15. A small cake with fancy
    frosting   p e t _ _   _ _ _ _

"MAN"HUNT

Each phrase below is a clue for an answer that contains the letters m a n.

1. A feeding trough for cattle   m a n _ _ _
2. A small orange   m a n _ _ _ _ _
3. A shelf above a fireplace   m a n _ _ _
4. An opening to a sewer   m a n _ _ _ _
5. A model for displaying clothes   m a n _ _ _ _ _ _
6. To treat roughly   m a n _ _ _ _ _
7. A province in Canada   M a n _ _ _ _ _
8. A stringed musical instrument   m a n _ _ _ _ _
9. A tropical fruit   m a n _ _
10. A large house   m a n _ _ _ _
11. Treatment for fingernails   m a n _ _ _ _ _
12. To make by hand or by machine   m a n _ _ _ _ _ _ _ _ _
13. Person in charge   m a n _ _ _ _
14. Numerous   m a n _
15. A large insect   _ _ _ _ _ _ _

    m a n _ _ _

"GO" TEAM "GO"

**Each phrase below is a clue for an answer that contains the letters
g o.**

1. A rodent   g o _ _ _ _

2. An outdoor sport   g o _ _

3. Stew   g o _ _ _ _

4. A boat with high pointed ends,
   used on the canals in Venice.   g o _ _ _ _ _

5. To make a mistake   g o _ _

6. Kind and generous   g o _ _ - _ _ _ _ _ _ _

7. To eat hurriedly   g o _ _ _ _

8. A dance   _ _ _ g o

9. An ape   g o _ _ _ _ _

10. To rule with authority   g o _ _ _ _

11. A drinking glass with a stem   g o _ _ _ _

12. Beautiful; magnificent   g o _ _ _ _ _

13. A toy on which one can hop
    from place to place   _ _ g o _ _ _ _ _

14. An end or aim one tries to
    achieve   g o _ _

15. Protective eyeglasses   g o _ _ _ _ _

SCRAMBLED "EGGS"

Each phrase below is a clue for an answer that contains the letters
e g g.

1. Being part of a group   _ e _ _ _ g _ _ g

2. The start   _ e g _ _ _ _ _ g

3. Searching   _ _ _ e _ _ _ g _ _ _ _ g

4. To overstate   e _ _ g g _ _ _ _ _

5. To give unwillingly   _ e g _ _ _ g _

6. A covering for the legs   _ e g g _ _ _ _

7. Careless   _ e g _ _ g _ _ _ _

8. A promise of marriage   e _ g _ g _ _ _ _ _

9. Promising; vowing   _ _ e _ g _ _ g

10. A large, dark purple vegetable   e g g _ _ _ _ _

11. A young bird ready to fly   _ _ e _ g _ _ _ g

12. To set apart   _ e g _ _ g _ _ _

13. Concerning   _ e g _ _ _ _ g

14. A winter holiday drink   e g g _ _ _

15. A utensil with revolving blades   e g g _ _ _ _ _ _

       used to beat and mix foods

E-D-U-C-A-T-I-O-N

List all the words you can make from the letters in EDUCATION.
(Note: All the words in your list must have at least 3 letters, and
each letter can be used only once in each word.)

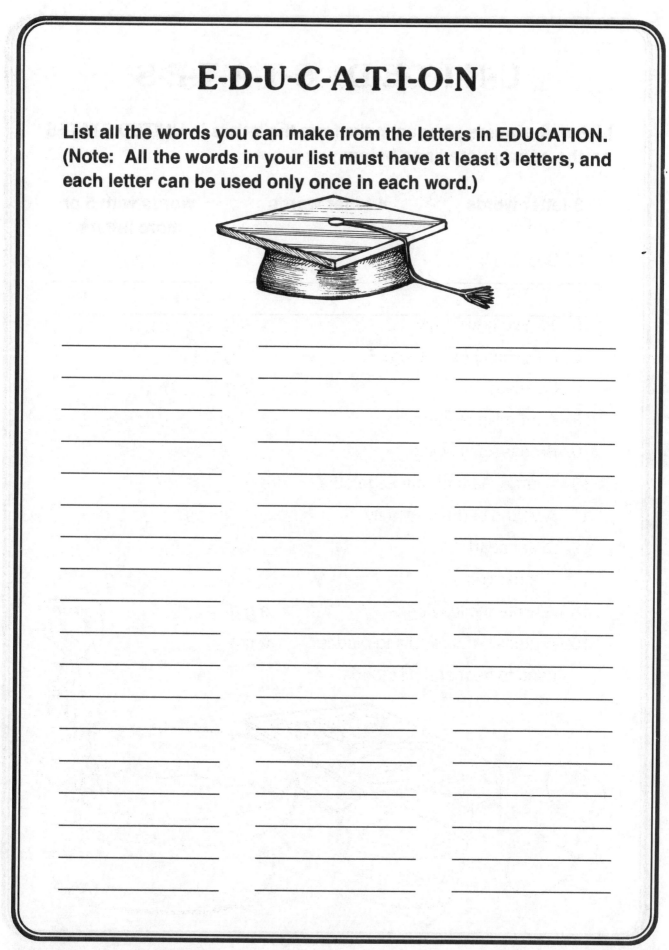

U-N-I-T-E-D S-T-A-T-E-S

List all the words you can make from the letters in UNITED STATES on the appropriate lines below.

3-letter words	4-letter words	words with 5 or more letters
_____	_____	_____
_____	_____	_____
_____	_____	_____
_____	_____	_____
_____	_____	_____
_____	_____	_____
_____	_____	_____
_____	_____	_____
_____	_____	_____
_____	_____	_____
_____	_____	_____
_____	_____	_____
_____	_____	_____
_____	_____	_____
_____	_____	_____
_____	_____	_____
_____	_____	_____
_____	_____	_____

WHERE IN THE UNITED STATES?

Find the letters in the words UNITED STATES to write the answers to the following clues.

1. A female relative   _ _ _ _
2. An exam   _ _ _ _
3. Past tense of eat   _ _ _
4. To join together   _ _ _ _ _
5. Five plus five   _ _ _
6. To rise to one's feet   _ _ _ _ _
7. To sample a food   _ _ _ _ _
8. A body of water   _ _ _
9. A lodging for campers   _ _ _ _
10. To be in want of   _ _ _ _
11. Earth's source of energy   _ _ _
12. The home of a lion   _ _ _
13. A large sea fish   _ _ _ _
14. A place to sit   _ _ _ _
15. Tiny grains on the beach   _ _ _ _
16. A piece of music   _ _ _ _
17. When the sun goes down   _ _ _ _ _ _
18. To be present at   _ _ _ _ _ _
19. To make fun of in a playful or unkind way   _ _ _ _ _
20. To finish   _ _ _

AROUND AND AROUND YOU GO

Starting with the letter "E," write every third letter around the box on the lines below. The result will be a famous proverb.

E A _ _ _ _ _ _ _ _ , _ _ _ _ _ _ _ _ _ ,

_ _ _ _ _ _ _ _ _ _ _ _ _ _ , _ _ _ _ _ _ ,

_ _ _ _ _ _ .

A PUZZLING PROVERB

Fill in the answers to the following clues. Then transfer the letters to the corresponding numbered blanks to reveal a famous proverb.

1. Earth's natural satellite

$\overline{}\ \overline{}\ \overline{}\ \overline{}$
25 16 23   8

2. A pronoun

$\overline{}\ \overline{}$
29 27

3. A primary color

$\overline{}\ \overline{}\ \overline{}\ \overline{}\ \overline{}\ \overline{}$
18 40   4 24 37 28

4. A foot covering

$\overline{}\ \overline{}\ \overline{}\ \overline{}$
11 33   2 26

5. A lot of small bubbles

$\overline{}\ \overline{}\ \overline{}\ \overline{}$
 1 22 13 35

6. On one occasion only

$\overline{}\ \overline{}\ \overline{}\ \overline{}$
 3 17   9 31

7. To approach

$\overline{}\ \overline{}\ \overline{}\ \overline{}$
30   7 39   6

8. Silent; saying nothing

$\overline{}\ \overline{}\ \overline{}$
14 20   5

9. An enthusiastic admirer

$\overline{}\ \overline{}\ \overline{}$
21 34 38

10. To look

$\overline{}\ \overline{}\ \overline{}$
32 10 15

11. A garden tool

$\overline{}\ \overline{}\ \overline{}$
12 19 36

$\overline{}\ \overline{}\ \overline{}\ \overline{}\ \ \overline{}\ \overline{}\ \ \overline{}\ \overline{}\ \overline{}\ \overline{}$,
 1   2   3   4   5   6   7   8   9 10

$\overline{}\ \overline{}\ \overline{}\ \overline{}\ \overline{}\ \ \overline{}\ \overline{}\ \ \overline{}\ \overline{}\ \overline{}$.
11 12 13 14 15   16 17   18 19 20

$\overline{}\ \overline{}\ \overline{}\ \overline{}\ \ \overline{}\ \overline{}\ \ \overline{}\ \overline{}\ \overline{}\ \overline{}\ \overline{}$,
21 22 23 24   25 26   27 28 29 30 31

$\overline{}\ \overline{}\ \overline{}\ \overline{}\ \overline{}\ \ \overline{}\ \overline{}\ \ \overline{}\ \overline{}$.
32 33 34 35 36   37 38   39 40

ANOTHER PUZZLING PROVERB

Fill in the answers to the following clues. Then transfer the letters to the corresponding numbered blanks to reveal a famous proverb.

1. Plural of this

  ___ ___ ___ ___ ___
  29 34 22 7   40

2. To throw without force

  ___ ___ ___ ___
  33 16 14 37

3. Australian tree-climbing animal

  ___ ___ ___ ___ ___
  18 27 6   15 12

4. Information about recent events

  ___ ___ ___ ___
  24 3   11 8

5. Feeling regret

  ___ ___ ___ ___ ___
  19 32 36 5   13

6. To keep out of sight

  ___ ___ ___ ___
  2   38 39 23

7. By preference

  ___ ___ ___ ___ ___ ___
  21 9   1   30 35 26

8. Solitary

  ___ ___ ___ ___
  10 17 28 25

9. Food prepared scrambled or
   over easy

  ___ ___ ___
  31 20 4

  ___ ___ ___   ___ ___ ___ ___ ___
  1   2   3   4   5   6   7   8

  ___ ___ ___ ___ ___ ___   ___ ___ ___ ___ ___
  9   10 11 12 13 14   15 16 17 18 19

  ___ ___ ___ ___ ___ ___ ___   ___ ___
  20 21 22 23 24 25 26   27 28

  ___ ___ ___   ___ ___ ___ ___ ___   ___ ___ ___ ___
  29 30 31   32 33 34 35 36   37 38 39 40

CODED MESSAGE

Answer each question below. Then use the code to reveal a famous proverb.

$\underline{\hphantom{8}}\ \underline{\hphantom{11}}\quad\ \underline{\hphantom{8}}\ \underline{\hphantom{6}}\ \underline{\hphantom{6}}\ \underline{\hphantom{1}}\ \underline{\hphantom{9}}\quad\ \underline{\hphantom{8}}$
8   11   8   6   6   1   9   8

$\underline{\hphantom{3}}\ \underline{\hphantom{8}}\ \underline{\hphantom{2}}\quad\ \underline{\hphantom{12}}\ \underline{\hphantom{9}}\ \underline{\hphantom{9}}\ \underline{\hphantom{6}}\ \underline{\hphantom{10}}\quad\ \underline{\hphantom{5}}\ \underline{\hphantom{14}}\ \underline{\hphantom{9}}$
3   8   2   12   9   9   6   10   5   14   9

$\underline{\hphantom{3}}\ \underline{\hphantom{13}}\ \underline{\hphantom{15}}\ \underline{\hphantom{5}}\ \underline{\hphantom{13}}\ \underline{\hphantom{7}}\quad\ \underline{\hphantom{8}}\ \underline{\hphantom{4}}\ \underline{\hphantom{8}}\ \underline{\hphantom{2}}$.
3   13   15   5   13   7   8   4   8   2

1. If 8 x 9 = 72, circle L. If it doesn't, circle U.
2. If the Atlantic Ocean is west of the U.S., circle V. If it is east of the U.S., circle Y.
3. If lime is a shade of green, circle D. If it isn't, circle M.
4. If Hawaii is an island, circle W. If it is a peninsula, circle K.
5. If synonyms are words that mean the opposite, circle L. If they aren't, circle T.
6. If the Statue of Liberty was given to us by England, circle B. If it wasn't, circle P.
7. If a telescope is used to view things far away, circle R. If it isn't, circle S.
8. If Robert E. Lee was a Confederate general, circle A. If he was a Union general, circle O.
9. If Canada is a state in the U.S., circle O. If it is a country in North America, circle E.
10. If 6 x 8 + 2 is equal to 10 x 5, circle S. If it isn't, circle R.
11. If America was named after Christopher Columbus, circle O. If it was named after Amerigo Vespucci, circle N.
12. If south paws are people who write left-handed, circle K. If they write right-handed, circle W.
13. If an octagon has 6 sides, circle I. If it has 8 sides, circle O.
14. If Ronald Reagan was once a movie star, circle H. If he wasn't, circle K.
15. If IX means 11 in Roman numerals, circle J. If it means 9, circle C.

HIDDEN ANIMALS

Hidden in each sentence is the name of an animal. Each can be found either in the middle of a word or by combining the end of one word with the beginning of the next. Underline the animal name in each sentence. An example has been done for you.

To and <u>fro g</u>oes the pendulum.

1. Goran came late to the party.

2. They do good work.

3. I can go at 6:30.

4. Steffi should be pleased with the results.

5. Magnus ate a whole bowl of popcorn.

6. Please allow me to help you.

7. We will leave for the picnic at noon.

8. She can't stand to be around cigarette smoke.

9. The teacher made Ernie stay after school.

10. Sheryl, I only have 50 cents in my pocket.

11. Sarah entered the church quietly.

12. Try some of these green grapes.

13. Is Mr. Roy Stern our new teacher?

14. They abhor senseless violence.

15. Cedric owns a sporting goods store.

DOUBLE LETTERS

Each phrase below is a clue for an answer that contains consecutive double letters.

Shawna Vasco
95882 Puriton Cr.
Huntington Bc. CA
92647

1. The writing on an envelope that shows where it should be sent

   _____

2. A farewell _____

3. A small pool of water _____

4. One who keeps a record of business accounts _____

5. A greeting _____

6. One who leads a parade, twirling a baton _____

7. Result produced by a cause _____

8. Joyful, glad _____

9. The dead body of an animal _____

10. Someone who tosses trash in public areas _____

11. To talk too much; chatter _____

12. Awful _____

13. Sport in which only the goalkeeper's hands may touch the ball

    _____

14. Opposite of defense _____

15. A courier _____

DOUBLE "OO" RANCH

Each phrase below is a clue for an answer that contains "oo."

1. An overabundance of water _____

2. To prepare food using heat _____

3. What we get from sheep _____

4. A favorite snack _____

5. Things we eat _____

6. A place to swim _____

7. Antonym for warm _____

8. Utensil used to eat soup _____

9. The part of a home where you sleep _____

10. Unit of measure, larger than an inch _____

11. A place where animals are kept _____

12. Sounds cows make _____

13. A train whistle _____

14. To see _____

15. A kind of dog _____

16. A farm animal _____

17. A pain in the mouth _____

18. A device used in weaving _____

19. The part of a car that covers the engine _____

20. An instrument, like a hammer, used to do work _____

64

BEGIN AND END

Each phrase below is a clue for an answer that begins and ends with the same letter.

1. Antonym of low   h _ _ h

2. A type of boat   k _ _ _ k

3. The most abundant gas in
   the atmosphere   n _ _ _ _ _ _ n

4. Children's sidewalk game   h _ _ _ _ _ _ _ h

5. The loss of memory   a _ _ _ _ _ a

6. Opposite of minimum   m _ _ _ _ _ m

7. Payment to stockholders   d _ _ _ _ _ _ d

8. A gas used in lighted signs   n _ _ n

9. One TV show in a series   e _ _ _ _ _ e

10. The fireplace floor   h _ _ _ _ h

11. Blue-green   a _ _ a

12. A small infant   n _ _ _ _ _ n

13. A ray of moonlight   m _ _ _ _ _ _ m

14. A place for performances   a _ _ _ a

15. One who forms opinions and
    gives judgments   c _ _ _ _ c

16. A continent   A _ _ _ _ _ _ _ _ a

17. Another continent   A _ _ _ _ _ _ _ a

18. Another continent   A _ _ _ _ a

19. Another continent   A _ _ a

20. Another continent   E _ _ _ _ e

A . . . . A TO Z . . . . Z

Brainstorm words that begin and end with the same letter.

a . . . a   _____   _____   _____

b . . . b   _____   _____   _____

c . . . c   _____   _____   _____

d . . . d   _____   _____   _____

e . . . e   _____   _____   _____

f . . . f   _____   _____   _____

g . . . g   _____   _____   _____

h . . . h   _____   _____   _____

i . . . i   _____   _____   _____

j . . . j   _____   _____   _____

k . . . k   _____   _____   _____

l . . . l   _____   _____   _____

m . . . m   _____   _____   _____

n . . . n   _____   _____   _____

o . . . o   _____   _____   _____

p . . . p   _____   _____   _____

q . . . q   _____   _____   _____

r . . . r   _____   _____   _____

s . . . s   _____   _____   _____

t . . . t   _____   _____   _____

u . . . u   _____   _____   _____

v . . . v   _____   _____   _____

w . . . w   _____   _____   _____

x . . . x   _____   _____   _____

y . . . y   _____   _____   _____

z . . . z   _____   _____   _____

A . . . . B

Write a word that begins with "a" and ends with "b." Continue
through the alphabet. Finish with a word that begins with "z"
and ends with "a."

a _____ b   n _____ o

b _____ c   o _____ p

c _____ d   p _____ q

d _____ e   q _____ r

e _____ f   r _____ s

f _____ g   s _____ t

g _____ h   t _____ u

h _____ i   u _____ v

i _____ j   v _____ w

j _____ k   w _____ x

k _____ l   x _____ y

l _____ m   y _____ z

m _____ n   z _____ a

WHAT'S TO EAT?

List food items that begin with each letter of the alphabet.

A _____ _____ _____

B _____ _____ _____

C _____ _____ _____

D _____ _____ _____

E _____ _____ _____

F _____ _____ _____

G _____ _____ _____

H _____ _____ _____

I _____ _____ _____

J _____ _____ _____

K _____ _____ _____

L _____ _____ _____

M _____ _____ _____

N _____ _____ _____

O _____ _____ _____

P _____ _____ _____

Q _____ _____ _____

R _____ _____ _____

S _____ _____ _____

T _____ _____ _____

U _____ _____ _____

V _____ _____ _____

W _____ _____ _____

X _____ _____ _____

Y _____ _____ _____

Z _____ _____ _____

BACK TO SCHOOL

List words related to school that begin with each letter of the alphabet.

A _____ _____ _____

B _____ _____ _____

C _____ _____ _____

D _____ _____ _____

E _____ _____ _____

F _____ _____ _____

G _____ _____ _____

H _____ _____ _____

I _____ _____ _____

J _____ _____ _____

K _____ _____ _____

L _____ _____ _____

M _____ _____ _____

N _____ _____ _____

O _____ _____ _____

P _____ _____ _____

Q _____ _____ _____

R _____ _____ _____

S _____ _____ _____

T _____ _____ _____

U _____ _____ _____

V _____ _____ _____

W _____ _____ _____

X _____ _____ _____

Y _____ _____ _____

Z _____ _____ _____

WHAT DOES IT MEAN?

Match each definition with a word from the word box.

1. Able to use either hand equally well _____

2. Appetizer _____

3. To speak without preparation _____

4. The other way around _____

5. And the rest _____

6. A magician's trick words _____

7. An ill-assorted mixture _____

8. An especially irritating annoyance _____

9. A left-handed person _____

10. Wordy, pompous language _____

11. Till we meet again _____

12. The very best _____

13. Served with ice cream on top _____

14. A useless item _____

15. An international code signal of distress _____

WORD BOX

hodgepodge   crème de la crème   pet peeve   ad lib

white elephant   southpaw   hors d'oeuvre   SOS

vice versa   ambidextrous   à la mode   hocus-pocus

et cetera   gobbledygook   auf Wiedersehen

COMPLETE THE PHRASE

1. Knife, fork, and _____

2. Hop, skip, and _____

3. Ready, set, _____

4. Morning, noon, and _____

5. The butcher, the baker, _____

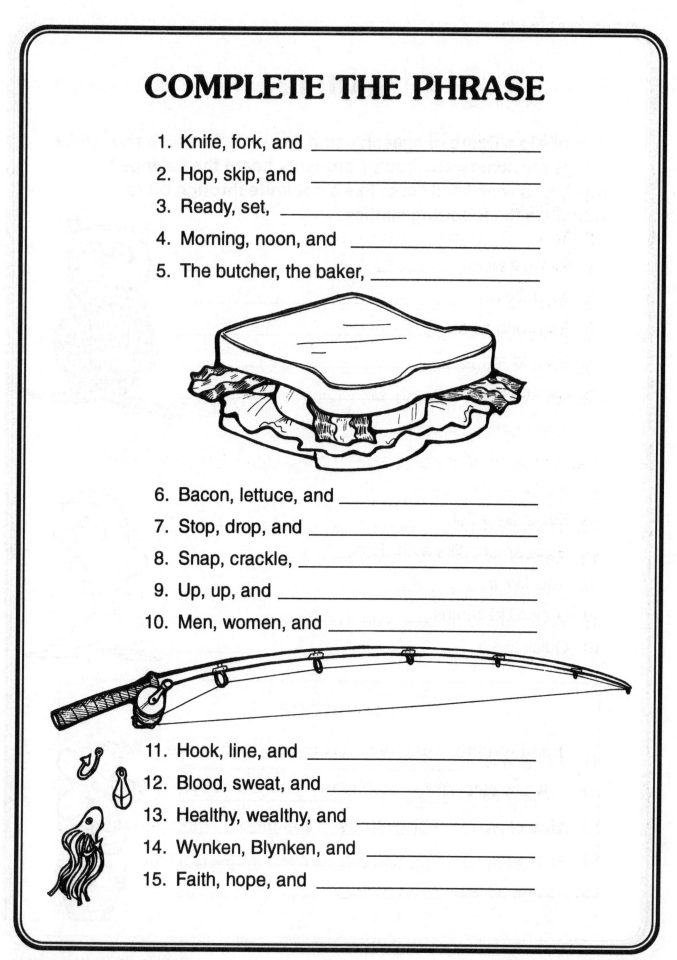

6. Bacon, lettuce, and _____

7. Stop, drop, and _____

8. Snap, crackle, _____

9. Up, up, and _____

10. Men, women, and _____

11. Hook, line, and _____

12. Blood, sweat, and _____

13. Healthy, wealthy, and _____

14. Wynken, Blynken, and _____

15. Faith, hope, and _____

SIMILES

A simile is a figure of speech using *like* or *as* in which two unlike things are compared. You've probably heard the sayings "as quick as a wink" and "cuts like a hot knife through butter." Complete the following similes.

1. As wise as an _____

2. As white as _____

3. As strong as an _____

4. As cold as _____

5. As cute as a _____

6. Feels like a fish _____

7. Runs around like a chicken _____

8. Eats like a _____

9. Drawn like moths _____

10. Quick like a _____

11. As fresh as a _____

12. As busy as a _____

13. As cool as a _____

14. As fit as a _____

15. As smooth as _____

PROVERBS

A proverb is an old, familiar saying. "Two wrongs don't make a right" is an example. Complete each of the following proverbs.

1. Variety is _____

2. If the shoe fits, _____

3. Don't judge a book _____

4. People who live in glass houses _____

5. Money is the root _____

6. All that glitters _____

7. Do unto others _____

8. You can lead a horse to water, _____

9. Be it ever so humble, _____

10. Curiosity _____

11. Never put off till tomorrow _____

12. A friend in need _____

13. Half a loaf _____

14. Two heads _____

15. Better late _____

16. Birds of a feather _____

17. Waste not _____

18. One picture is worth _____

19. He who hesitates _____

20. The early bird _____

IDIOMS

Idioms are expressions whose meanings are different from the literal ones. Explain what the idioms below actually mean.

1. When Angelica said, "That movie **took my breath away**," she meant _____

2. "When Dad finally **put his foot down**, my brother started to do better in school," said Boris. What Boris meant was _____ _____

3. Dana stood and said, "I guess I'll **hit the road** now." What Dana meant was _____

4. When Mario said that he was a bit **under the weather** last weekend, he meant that _____

5. When Nickoli said that he **slept like a log** last night, he meant _____

6. "I'll be **in the doghouse** for sure," exclaimed Roberto. What Roberto really meant was _____ _____

7. "**Hold your horses**," remarked the police officer. The police officer meant _____

8. When Ryan asked Patricia, "Are you **getting cold feet**?" he was actually asking _____

9. If Grandpa loves **to spin a yarn**, he _____ _____

10. When Leslie says that she is **in the dark** about what's going on, she means _____

ANALOGIES

**Analogies are comparisons. Complete each analogy below.
An example has been done for you.
Wide is to narrow as tall is to short.**

1. Big is to _____ as large is to small.

2. Hat is to head as shoe is to _____.

3. Bird is to nest as _____ is to hive.

4. Rug is to _____ as curtain is to window.

5. _____ is to road as boat is to lake.

6. Boy is to man as _____ is to woman.

7. _____ is to room as gate is to yard.

8. Sleep is to tired as _____ is to hungry.

9. Zoo is to animals as library is to _____.

10. Floor is to _____ as ceiling is to top.

11. _____ is to grass as blue is to sky.

12. Belt is to _____ as bracelet is to wrist.

13. Car is to driver as airplane is to _____.

14. Book is to _____ as television is to watch.

15. Grape is to vine as peach is to _____.

16. Ear is to hearing as _____ is to sight.

17. _____ is to day as dusk is to dawn.

18. Thanksgiving is to November as Christmas is to _____.

19. Calf is to cow as _____ is to lion.

20. _____ is to uncle as niece is to aunt.

ANSWER KEY

Page 3, FAMOUS PAIRS
Robin, Clark, Juliet, Dr. Jekyll, Tom, Superman, Cleopatra, Minnie, Ken, Jack, Popeye, Napoleon, Wilbur, Dagwood, Gretel.

Page 4, PICK A PAIR!
Answers will vary. Mittens, gloves, socks, shoes, sandals, slippers, ice skates, roller skates, skis, boots, shoelaces, jeans, shorts, pajamas, earrings, glasses, pliers, binoculars, scissors, dice.

Page 5, WORD PAIRS
1-chips. 2-tomato. 3-shine. 4-right. 5-cream. 6-seek. 7-dogs. 8-eggs. 9-puff. 10-out. 11-dandy. 12-pencil. 13-key. 14-white (or blue). 15-match. 16-quiet. 17-spice. 18-day. 19-soul. 20-pains. 21-joy. 22-order. 23-cranny. 24-baggage.

Page 7, ALL ALIKE
1-primary colors. 2-feelings. 3-milk products. 4-ways to move. 5-items with three of something. 6-odd numbers. 7-states. 8-means of transportation. 9-continents. 10-directions. 11-months with 30 days. 12-types of clouds. 13-poultry. 14-vegetables. 15-sleep furniture.

Page 8, WHICH ONE DOESN'T BELONG?
1-niece, male relatives. 2-math, reference books. 3-tomato, flowers. 4-chicken, animals with four legs. 5-eraser, writing tools. 6-kid, lion family. 7-sun, signs of bad weather. 8-green, primary colors. 9-watermelon, citrus fruits. 10-Cowboys, baseball teams. 11-cry, expressions of humor. 12-butter, grain products. 13-blood, body organs. 14-hot dogs, condiments. 15-Kansas, states that border the Pacific Ocean.

Page 9, THE GREAT ESCAPE
1-goat. 2-cow. 3-horse. 4-bull. 5-sheep. 6-pigs.

Page 10, BASEBALL LINEUP
1-Tom. 2-David. 3-Jordi. 4-Greg. 5-Andrei. 6-Marc. 7-Luis. 8-Phil. 9-Carlos.

Page 11, FAVORITE FOODS
Chicken-Jana. Hot dog-Michael. Pizza-Megan. Cheeseburger-Sergi.

Page 12, RICHEY'S DOG
1-collie. 2-dachshund. 3-cocker spaniel. 4-greyhound. 5-pug.

Page 13, BLACK OUT
GHOULAID.

Page 14, PALINDROME WORD FIND

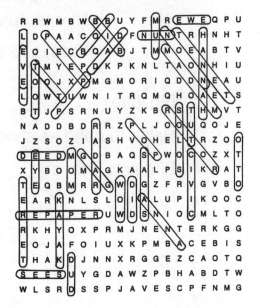

Page 15, SCHOOL DAYS WORD FIND

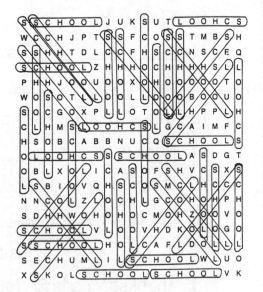

ANSWER KEY (continued)

Page 16, ANIMAL WORD FIND

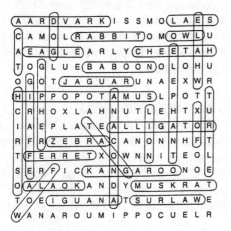

Page 17, MIXED FRUIT

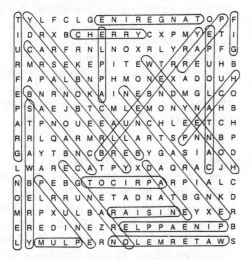

Page 18, CARS, CARS, AND MORE CARS

Page 19, SHADOWS

1-bicycle. 2-bird on a branch. 3-slide. 4-umbrella. 5-swing. 6-Statue of Liberty.

Page 22, HIDDEN MEANINGS

1-three degrees below zero. 2-split level. 3-uptown. 4-pair of dice. 5-sandbox. 6-small pox. 7-business before pleasure. 8-just between you and me. 9-reading between the lines. 10-head over heels. 11-backward glance. 12-I understand.

Page 23, MORE HIDDEN MEANINGS

1-You're under arrest. 2-order in the court. 3-age before beauty. 4-face to face. 5-highchair. 6-hand in hand. 7-skating on thin ice. 8-crossroads. 9-mind over matter. 10-downtown. 11-pie in the face. 12-good afternoon.

Page 24, HOW MANY?

1-5. 2-13. 3-20. 4-16. 5-88. 6-10. 7-206. 8-500. 9-50. 10-132. 11-24. 12-100. 13-64. 14-11. 15-5.

Page 25, ADDITION & SUBTRACTION

1. $3 + 2 - 1 + 4 - 1 + 3 = 10$
2. $8 - 7 + 1 + 4 + 4 - 6 = 4$
3. $5 + 3 - 2 + 4 - 1 + 5 = 14$
4. $2 - 1 + 8 + 9 - 3 + 5 = 20$
5. $5 - 3 + 4 - 4 - 2 + 9 = 9$
6. $7 - 6 + 2 + 9 - 9 - 3 = 0$
7. $4 + 9 - 3 + 7 + 3 - 1 = 19$
8. $9 - 8 + 6 + 3 - 5 + 1 = 6$
9. $3 + 5 - 3 + 9 - 6 + 5 = 13$
10. $5 - 1 - 1 + 3 + 4 + 7 = 17$

Page 26, NUMERAL-INITIAL EQUATIONS

1-1 voice in a solo. 2-2 pints in a quart. 3-3 teaspoons in a tablespoon. 4-4 quarts in a gallon. 5-5 toes on a foot. 6-9 players on a baseball team. 7-9 planets in the solar system. 8-12 eggs in a dozen. 9-16 tablespoons in a cup. 10-36 inches in a yard. 11-50 states in the United States. 12-66 books in the Bible. 13-88 keys on a piano. 14-144 items in a gross. 15-206 bones in your body. 16-360 degrees in a circle. 17- 640 acres in a square mile. 18-1000 milliliters in a liter. 19-2000 pounds in a ton. 20-5280 feet in a mile.

#490 Brain Teasers • Intermediate

ANSWER KEY (continued)

Page 27, CHANGE PLEASE!
1-4 quarters. 2-3 quarters, 1 dime, 3 nickels.
3-7 dimes, 6 nickels. 4-1 half dollar, 2 quarters.
5-3 quarters, 5 nickels. 6-6 dimes, 5 nickels, 15
pennies. 7-1 half dollar, 1 quarter, 2 dimes, 1
nickel. 8-3 quarters, 2 dimes, 1 nickel.
9-10 dimes **or** 1 quarter, 6 dimes, 3 nickels.
10-1 half dollar, 1 quarter, 1 dime, 1 nickel, 10
pennies.

Page 28, TIMELY CHORE
1-millisecond, one one-thousandth of a second.
2-second, 1000 milliseconds. 3-minute, 60 seconds.
4-hour, 60 minutes. 5-day, 24 hours. 6-week,
7 days. 7-fortnight, 2 weeks. 8-month 28 to 31
days or one-twelfth of a year. 9-year, 12 months.
10-decade, 10 years. 11-score, 20 years.
12-century, 100 years. 13-millennium, 1000 years.

Page 29, NAMES AND NUMBERS
1-Grumpy, Happy, Doc, Dopey, Sneezy, Sleepy,
Bashful. 2-George Washington, Abraham
Lincoln, Thomas Jefferson, Theodore Roosevelt.
3-sight, hearing, touch, taste, smell. 4-Virginia,
Massachusetts, New Hampshire, New York,
Connecticut, Maryland, Rhode Island, Delaware,
Pennsylvania, North Carolina, New Jersey,
South Carolina, Georgia. 5-Dasher, Dancer,
Prancer, Vixen, Comet, Cupid, Donner, Blitzen,
Rudolph. 6-Mercury, Venus. 7-violet, blue,
green, yellow, orange, red. 8-New York City,
Philadelphia, Washington, D.C. 9-Alberta, British
Columbia, Manitoba, New Brunswick,
Newfoundland, Nova Scotia, Ontario, Prince
Edward Island, Quebec, Saskatchewan,
Northwest Territories, Yukon Territory.
10-Mercury, Venus, Earth, Mars, Jupiter, Saturn,
Uranus, Neptune, Pluto.

Page 31, DO YOU KNOW?
1-left. 2-Susan B. Anthony. 3-bottom. 4-hot.
5-George Washington. 6-John F. Kennedy.
7-George Washington, Benjamin Franklin.
8-Mt. Everest. 9-on the Statue of Liberty.
10-break it open for the goodies inside.

Page 32, GENERAL TRIVIA
1-six. 2-Abraham Lincoln. 3-buffalo. 4-red,
yellow. 5-peacock. 6-escalator. 7-every four
years. 8-once upon a time. 9-captain.
10-autumn. 11-sheep. 12-go under water.

Page 33, TALLEST, LARGEST, FASTEST
1-redwood tree. 2-Sears Tower. 3-Mt. Everest.
4-Greenland. 5-Asia. 6-anaconda. 7-North
African ostrich. 8-African bush elephant.
9-blue whale. 10-peregrine falcon. 11-cheetah.
12-killer whale.

Page 34, PATRIOTIC TRIVIA
1-Capitol. 2-White House. 3-Potomac. 4-seven.
5-Old Glory **or** Stars and Stripes. 6-executive,
legislative, judicial. 7-In God We Trust. 8-"The
Star-Spangled Banner." 9-bald eagle. 10-six
years. 11-for life or until retirement. 12-Bill of
Rights. 13-1800. 14-John Adams. 15-nickel.

Page 35, PRESIDENTIAL TRIVIA
1-James Buchanan. 2-John Adams. 3-William
Henry Harrison. 4-John Quincy Adams.
5-Benjamin Harrison. 6-Richard Nixon.
7-Franklin D. Roosevelt. 8-Gerald Ford.
9-Thomas Jefferson. 10-George Washington.
11-James Madison. 12-Abraham Lincoln.
13-John F. Kennedy. 14-Andrew Jackson.
15-Dwight D. Eisenhower.

Page 36, SOCIAL STUDIES TRIVIA
1-east. 2-island. 3-Mississippi. 4-atlas. 5-Michigan.
6-Niña, Pinta, Santa Maria. 7-France. 8-Amerigo
Vespucci. 9-Philadelphia. 10-John Wilkes Booth.
11-San Antonio, Texas. 12-1861 - 1865.
13-Declaration of Independence. 14-Britain and
the United States. 15-Neil Armstrong.

Page 37, SCIENCE TRIVIA
1-thermometer. 2-nervous system. 3-heart beat.
4-invertebrate. 5-gills. 6-oysters. 7-fossils.
8-telescope. 9-Jupiter. 10-orbit. 11-moon.
12-Halley's Comet. 13-galaxy. 14-solid, liquid,
gas. 15-barometer.

Page 38, ENGLISH TRIVIA
1-adverbs. 2-Charlotte. 3-author. 4-fiction.
5-Judy Blume. 6-Aesop. 7-autobiography.
8-Samuel Clemens. 9-synonyms. 10-*Little
Women.* 11-nonfiction. 12-noun. 13-subject,
predicate. 14-apostrophe. 15-Beverly Cleary.

Page 39, PALINDROMES
1-tot. 2-dad **or** pop. 3-mom. 4-Anna **or** Hannah.
5-Bob. 6-solos. 7-pop. 8-peep. 9-level. 10-kayak.
11-ewe. 12-bib. 13-eye. 14-toot. 15-pup. 16-did.
17-deed. 18-gag. 19-dud. 20-civic.

ANSWER KEY (continued)

Page 40, ABBREVIATIONS
1-street. 2-cash (or collect) on delivery. 3-building.
4-pounds. 5-post office. 6-miscellaneous. 7-ounce.
8-before noon. 9-package. 10-I owe you.
11-highway. 12-department. 13-miles per hour.
14-not available. 15-vice president. 16-as soon
as possible. 17-manufacturing. 18-Bachelor of
Arts. 19-self-addressed stamped envelope.
20-and so forth. 21-railroad. 22-District Attorney.
23-chief executive officer. 24-Doctor of
Medicine. 25-please answer. 26-for example.
27-before Christ. 28-cardio-pulmonary resuscita-
tion. 29-for your information. 30-especially.

Page 42, RHYMING WORD PAIRS
1-fat cat. 2-soggy doggy **or** wet pet. 3-glad lad.
4-rude dude. 5-sad dad. 6-cross boss. 7-bad lad.
8-Swiss miss. 9-lazy daisy. 10-bony pony.
11-shy fly. 12-bright light. 13-mouse house.
14-no dough. 15-funny money. 16-double trouble.
17-bug's mug. 18-big pig. 19-long song.
20-late date.

Page 43, WORD CHAIN
1-Honolulu. 2-lunch. 3-church. 4-chum.
5-umbrella. 6-lattice. 7-centimeter. 8-erosion.
9-once-over. 10-erase. 11-season. 12-once.
13-century. 14-Ryan. 15-answer. 16-eradicate.
17-tempo. 18-poncho. 19-Honolulu.

Page 45, WORD WINDERS
1-cold. 2-colt. 3-bolt. 4-bold. 5-bald. 6-ball.
7-bell. 8-belt. 9-melt. 10-molt.11-mold. 12-mole.
13-hole. 14-hold. 15-gold. 16-fold. 17-food.
18-fool. 19-tool. 20-pool.

Page 46, ONE WORD PLUS ANOTHER
1-son, net, sonnet. 2-rat, tan, rattan. 3-pea, nut,
peanut. 4-men, ace, menace. 5-sea, son,
season. 6-Jack, son, Jackson. 7-off, ice, office.
8-dam, pen, dampen. 9-cot, ton, cotton. 10-sun,
dry, sundry.

Page 47, WHAT'S THE MESSAGE?
1-peanuts. 2-authors. 3-braille. 4-skating.
5-Penguin. 6-senator. 7-New Deal. 8-redhead.
9-emperor. 10-aviator. 11-monster. 12-prophet.
13-pianist. 14-villain. 15-general.

Page 48, "CORN"-FED WORDS
1-corncob. 2-cornea. 3-corncrib. 4-corny.
5-corner. 6-cornet. 7-corned beef. 8-cut corners.

9-cornflakes. 10-cornstarch. 11-corn oil.
12-cornerstone. 13-cornice. 14-cornerback.
15-cornucopia.

Page 49, "FAR" OUT
1-farewell. 2-farm hand. 3-faraway. 4-farm team.
5-farthing. 6-farmer. 7-far-fetched. 8-far-reaching.
9-fare. 10-farce. 11-to go too far. 12-so far so
good. 13-farther. 14-Far East. 15-farrow.

Page 50, THIS "ORE" THAT
1-Oregon. 2-chore. 3-forest. 4-snore. 5-more.
6-oregano. 7-carnivores. 8-galore. 9-forefinger.
10-ignore. 11-forecast. 12-adore. 13-forefather.
14-swore. 15-shore.

Page 51, "PET" PEEVES
1-petal. 2-petite. 3-carpet. 4-petunia. 5-petroleum.
6-petrified. 7-petticoat. 8-petition. 9-petty officer.
10-puppet. 11-petty cash. 12-repetitious.
13-Peter. 14-petri dish. 15-petit four.

Page 52, "MAN"HUNT
1-manger. 2-mandarin. 3-mantel. 4-manhole.
5-mannequin. 6-manhandle. 7-Manitoba.
8-mandolin. 9-mango. 10-mansion.
11-manicure. 12-manufacture. 13-manager.
14-many. 15-praying mantis.

Page 53, "GO" TEAM "GO"
1-gopher. 2-golf. 3-goulash. 4-gondola. 5-goof.
6-good-hearted. 7-gobble. 8-tango. 9-gorilla.
10-govern. 11-goblet. 12-gorgeous. 13-pogo
stick. 14-goal. 15-goggles.

Page 54, SCRAMBLED "EGGS"
1-belonging. 2-beginning. 3-investigating.
4-exaggerate. 5-begrudge. 6-leggings.
7-negligent. 8-engagement. 9-pledging.
10-eggplant. 11-fledgling. 12-segregate.
13-regarding. 14-eggnog. 15-eggbeater.

Page 57, WHERE IN THE UNITED STATES?
1-aunt. 2-test. 3-ate. 4-unite. 5-ten. 6-stand.
7-taste. 8-sea. 9-tent. 10-need. 11-sun. 12-den.
13-tuna. 14-seat. 15-sand. 16-tune. 17-sunset.
18-attend. 19-tease. 20-end.

Page 58, AROUND AND AROUND YOU GO
Early to bed, early to rise, makes a man healthy,
wealthy, and wise.

ANSWER KEY (continued)

Page 59, A PUZZLING PROVERB
1-moon. 2-it. 3-yellow. 4-shoe. 5-foam. 6-once. 7-come. 8-mum. 9-fan. 10-see. 11-hoe. Fool me once, shame on you. Fool me twice, shame on me.

Page 60, ANOTHER PUZZLING PROVERB
1-these. 2-toss. 3-koala. 4-news. 5-sorry. 6-hide. 7-rather. 8-lone. 9-egg. The grass always looks greener on the other side.

Page 61, CODED MESSAGE
1-L. 2-Y. 3-D. 4-W. 5-T. 6-P. 7-R. 8-A. 9-E. 10-S. 11-N. 12-K. 13-O. 14-H. 15-C. An apple a day keeps the doctor away.

Page 62, HIDDEN ANIMALS
1-camel. 2-dog. 3-goat. 4-fish. 5-owl. 6-seal. 7-cat. 8-bear. 9-deer. 10-lion. 11-hen. 12-ape. 13-oyster. 14-horse. 15-cow.

Page 63, DOUBLE LETTERS
1-Address. 2-good-by. 3-puddle. 4-bookkeeper. 5-hello. 6-majorette. 7-effect. 8-happy. 9-carcass. 10-litterbug. 11-babble. 12-terrible. 13-soccer. 14-offense. 15-messenger.

Page 64, DOUBLE "OO" RANCH
1-flood. 2-cook. 3-wool. 4-cookie. 5-food. 6-pool. 7-cool. 8-spoon. 9-bedroom. 10-foot. 11-zoo. 12-moo. 13-toot. 14-look. 15-poodle. 16-rooster. 17-toothache. 18-loom. 19-hood. 20-tool.

Page 65, BEGIN AND END
1-high. 2-kayak. 3-nitrogen. 4-hopscotch. 5-amnesia. 6-maximum. 7-dividend. 8-neon. 9-episode. 10-hearth. 11-aqua. 12-newborn. 13-moonbeam. 14-arena. 15-critic. 16-Antarctica. 17-Australia. 18-Africa. 19-Asia. 20-Europe.

Page 66, A . . . . A TO Z . . . . Z
Answers will vary. area, bomb, classic, dread, evade, fluff, going, health, iambi, kick, liberal, maximum, noon, overdo, peep, radar, stress, trumpet, unau, vav, window, Xerox, yummy, zizz.

Page 67, A . . . . B
Answers will vary. absorb, basic, cold, divorce, elf, flag, graph, Hawaii, junk, kill, legalism, melon, no, overlap, queer, recess, street, tableau, UV, view, wax, x-ray, zebra.

Page 70, WHAT DOES IT MEAN?
1-ambidextrous. 2-hors d'oeuvre. 3-ad lib. 4-vice versa. 5-et cetera. 6-hocus-pocus. 7-hodgepodge. 8-pet peeve. 9-southpaw. 10-gobbledygook. 11-auf Wiedersehen. 12-crème de la crème. 13-à la mode. 14-white elephant. 15-SOS.

Page 71, COMPLETE THE PHRASE
1-spoon. 2-jump. 3-go. 4-night. 5-the candlestick maker. 6-tomato. 7-roll. 8-pop. 9-away. 10-children. 11-sinker. 12-tears. 13-wise. 14-Nod. 15-charity.

Page 72, SIMILES
1-owl. 2-snow **or** a sheet **or** a ghost.. 3-ox. 4-ice. 5-button. 6-out of water. 7-with its head cut off. 8-bird. 9-to a flame **or** to a light. 10-bunny. 11-daisy. 12-bee **or** beaver. 13-cucumber. 14-fiddle. 15-silk or glass.

Page 73, PROVERBS
1-the spice of life. 2-wear it. 3-by its cover. 4-shouldn't throw stones. 5-of all evil. 6-is not gold. 7-as you would have them do unto you. 8-but you can't make him drink. 9-there's no place like home. 10-killed the cat. 11-what you can do today. 12-is a friend indeed. 13-is better than none. 14-are better than one. 15-than never. 16-flock together. 17-want not. 18-a thousand words. 19-is lost. 20-catches the worm.

Page 74, IDIOMS
1-it scared or shocked her. 2-his father got serious and set rules or limits. 3-she was ready to leave. 4-he had not felt well. 5-he slept soundly. 6-he was going to be in trouble. 7- "Stop." 8- "Are you scared or changing your mind?" 9-loves to tell a story. 10-she doesn't know what is happening.

Page 75, ANALOGIES
1-little. 2-foot. 3-bee. 4-floor. 5-car. 6-girl. 7-door. 8-eat. 9-books. 10-bottom. 11-green. 12-waist. 13-pilot. 14-read. 15-tree. 16-eye. 17-night. 18-December. 19-cub. 20-nephew.